NO REST FOR THE WICKED

By

Oliver Seligman

The material in this book may not be reproduced or transmitted in whole or in part in any medium (whether electronic, mechanical or otherwise) without the express written authorization of Oliver Seligman (the publisher). To request authorization, please contact Oliver Seligman, outlining the specific material involved, the proposed medium, and if applicable, the number of copies, as well as the purpose of use.

All characters and events in this publication are fictitious and any resemblance to real persons, living or dead, is purely co-incidental.

BCCN 123456789

Copyright © Oliver Seligman 2018

Also, by Oliver Seligman

The Broker Who broke Free

Contents

Chapter 1	Ernie and the Ambulance	1
Chapter 2	Beauty and the Beast	28
Chapter 3	Mirror, mirror on the wall	47
Chapter 4	Half-wit	67
Chapter 5	Puppy Love	91
Chapter 6	Paradise Lost	116
Chapter 7	Betrayal	136
Chapter 8	Heart break	154
Chapter 9	Rex	166
Chapter 10	Russian Roulette	193
Chapter 11	Dr. Fritz	219

Ten years pass

Chapter 12	Mirror, mirror on the wall	232
Chapter 13	The Bunker	258
Chapter 14	Mission failed	274
Chapter 15	On the Lamb	288
Chapter 16	The End of Ernie	304
Chapter 17	On the Run	325

This book is dedicated to my father who loves to laugh, my mother who loves to love, and all those people who make us laugh.

CHAPTER 1

Ernie and the Ambulance

"So, Mr. Clark, can you tell the court why you were driving an ambulance with enough alcohol in your bloodstream to sedate a camel?" The lawyer smirked, clearly enjoying the prospect of roasting another defendant on a spit.

"Umm, well. There moost have been a mistake, like," Barry Clark, an ambulance driver from Newcastle replied, looking nervously at his hands. "Ah, umm, well, ah never tooched a drop, like. The breathalyser. It moost have been booggered… Oops," he mumbled, looking sheepishly at the lawyer. "Sorry your Honour. What ah meant to say was. The breathalyser was, boosted. Yes, yes, that's what ah meant your Highness, boosted, like."

It was a cold November morning in 1985 when the hit and run case finally came to court, nearly a year after the accident had occurred. Barry stood alone in the dock dressed in a cheap brown suit, his bleary eyes staring blankly ahead. He would be fifty-two this Christmas, which meant he was only three years away from early retirement and a glorious life in the South of Spain. Sunshine all year round, British pubs serving full English breakfasts, and free copies of *The Sun* for all their customers. It would be paradise.

As Barry's attention returned to the tall, thin, vulture of a man standing in front of him, he looked down at his hands once more. They were trembling. That morning he had tried to steady his nerves with half a bottle of gin, but it had not helped. He was still terrified; his mind battling between two stark choices. He could stick to his fictitious story, hoping it would get him off the hook, or he could come clean and avoid a deep sense of guilt that would suck the pleasure from those Spanish breakfasts. Barry was not a bad man but looking down the barrel of a prison sentence and a hefty fine, he decided honesty was not the best policy. So, he lied, and lied, and then lied some more. He might have got away with it had he actually been a good liar, or had he faced a prosecutor who was not so hungry for blood. Neither was the case. Barry had to undergo the ruthless cross-examination of a highflying upstart from London, who was determined to make a name for himself before graduating to the Bar. Right now, that upstart was in complete control and licking his lips in anticipation.

o o o

Ten months earlier in the spring of 1984, a teenager was wandering along a quiet, country road a few miles north of Newcastle. It was only ten o'clock in the morning, but the sun was already beating down on the solitary figure, threatening to burn the freckled skin on the back of his neck. Ernie Manning smiled as he enjoyed the quiet tranquility of his morning stroll. His GP had told him to take in some fresh air at least three times a week, and he had decided to follow this advice to the letter.

"It'll be good for your asthma and your health in general," his well-spoken doctor had reassured him, and the slightly built, sixteen-year-old redhead had hung on his every word. Ernie had a healthy respect for doctors, having had a great deal of contact with them over the years, out of misfortune rather than choice. The next morning, he took the bus to Hexham and set out on his first ever country amble. After all, what harm could possibly come from getting out in nature once in a while?

"Ah this is gre'at man, it's better than ah'd imagined, like," he thought in his soft Geordie lilt, as he took a couple of short breaths from his inhaler. Despite being of a nervous disposition and having a fear of open spaces, the doctor's suggestion seemed to be doing the trick.

Ernie did not get far before he needed to stop, and resting his hands on his hips, he took in the scenery that lay before him. The morning sun reflected off the calm surface of a woodland lake, rolling hills stretched far into the distance, and a small, brown rabbit hopped about on the heath in front of him. A heath which had seen the Celts, the Vikings, and more recently hundreds of drunken, quad-biking trips come and go, yet remained surprisingly serene. *"Northumbria really is God's country,"* he sighed contentedly. The whole experience was peaceful beyond words. The young man scratched the back of his head, oblivious to the flakes of dandruff that floated from his scalp. Then he glanced at his Mickey Mouse wristwatch, and with a hint of a spring in his step, he began to walk along the grassy verge heading nowhere in particular.

Ernie Manning was a simple soul who was not blessed with brains or good looks. His skin was pale, his front teeth bucked, and he was slightly stooped from a life believing he was less than other people. Yet today he walked a little taller than usual. Something had changed, something subtle but at the same time profound. Was it possible he was experiencing a taste of happiness? He was not sure, but it felt good to be alone with no-one to shout at him or shoulder charge him off the pavement. Ernie soon became mesmerised by the sight of his battered trainers landing on the soft earth one after the other. Amongst the fields and flowers, he felt no need to worry about the trivial matters which commonly occupied his mind and was filled with a deep sense of contentment. A contentment he cherished, because it was so extraordinarily unusual for him to experience such a state. Whenever good things happened to cross Ernie's path, which was not very often at all, his reaction was primarily one of suspicion. There was always a voice in the back of his head nagging away at him.

"*The good times never last,"* it whispered, and he would shudder. Right now, that voice was quiet, and its absence allowed him to feel a deep connection with everything around him. Today he was not going to think about his problems. Instead he continued to enjoy the sight of his trainers padding their way along the roadside, and the quiet aliveness of his silent mind.

At a quarter to eleven, Ernie spied a plant peering up at him from the other side of the road and stopped to take a better look.

"No, it can't be," he exclaimed. "That's, that's

loocky heather." At first glance the heather looked similar to the kind his mother put in vases at home, but this plant was far more beautiful and its white flowers somehow purer. "Ah don't believe it, like. Ah think ah've found me'self a sprig of loocky heather!" He exclaimed as he walked across the road to take a better look. It was unheard of for anyone except Gipsy soothsayers to find such a rare plant. Lucky heather just did not grow in places where ordinary people could discover it, and certainly not at the side of roads. This was quite something. This was, dare he think it, lucky. Ernie admired the beautiful plant and bent over to draw its sweet fragrance into his nostrils. This had to mean something. It had to be a sign. Perhaps sixteen years of misfortune was finally over?

o o o

"I am *not* your Honour, or your Highness, Mr. Clark. Your Honour is sitting over there in the wig, and as for Her Royal Highness? Well, I have no idea where Queen Elizabeth is, but she is most definitely not in this courtroom," the lawyer spat in a polished English accent, enjoying his own sarcasm a little too much. His lips curled into a snide expression as he spoke, as his eyes darted in anticipation of Barry's next blunder. An expensive three-piece suit hung from his broad but skeletal shoulders, and his long limbs and protruding elbows accentuating the threat he now posed to the ambulance driver's freedom.

"Ah've told ya," Barry insisted, "ah had not been drinking. Ah was as sober as a judge. Whoops, sorry your honour, no offence intended."

The judge ignored him.

"Getting back to my point, Mr. Clark. You claim the breathalyser was 'boosted', but how could you possibly know? You are not a technician and you have no training with this equipment, so please tell the court how exactly you knew it was," he paused for effect, "boosted." The lawyer's final word was full of contempt, and Barry could do nothing other than stare at him with a dazed expression on his face, like a rabbit caught in car headlights. "Do you know how many of these state-of-the-art breathalysers give faulty readings, Mr. Clark?" The lawyer continued before Barry had had time to answer his previous question. Barry shook his head. Those full English breakfasts were slipping away like sand through his fingers. "No? Well I shall enlighten you. Just under one ten thousandth of a percent. That's one in a million for those of us who prefer basic English. Which I imagine *you* do. Yet you claim the breathalyzer was boosted. How convenient."

"Well, ahh, umm..." Barry stammered, frantically searching the courtroom to find someone who could rescue him, but no-one could. His eyes finally came to rest on the ancient, wooden floor in front of him, where he hoped a Barry-sized hole would somehow appear and swallow him up.

o o o

There was not a lot of room inside the speeding blood wagon. What, with two paramedics, a six-foot vomiting tramp, and all the equipment they squeeze into ambulances, things were pretty cosy in the back. The ambulance crew were all too familiar with their foul-smelling passenger. Every month they drove him from his bench, under the rhododendron bushes in Hexham park, to the Faraday Hospital Psychiatric day unit in Newcastle. The paramedics were ordinary folk, dedicated to serving the local community and making an honest living. The tramp, on the other hand, was a complicated man. In his previous life he had been a well-respected curator at the Dalglish Art Gallery, but two failed marriages and an uncontrollable attraction to gin had left him both homeless and penniless. When sober the tramp was quite the gentleman; quiet, retiring and popular with the locals. He went about his business with a certain dignity and poise. However, as soon as he had had a few too many, he transformed into an overbearing sex pest. Today was a Tuesday, and as soon as he had woken up, he had decided to celebrate it by testing the strength of his constitution with a bottle of *Famous Grouse*. The seventy-year-old had enjoyed the testing procedure a great deal, but his constitution had not held up too well. His blood pressure had hit the roof, he had thrown up more times than he could count and then passed out. A dog walker had found him lying naked under his bench in the park and called an ambulance. The same ambulance that answered the same call every month.

Despite his challenges the tramp was an unusually positive man, and although the paramedics had fastened both of his wrists to a metal trolley, he was not the least bit disheartened. For some reason, the novelty of riding in an ambulance whilst wrapped up in a silver space blanket, never wore off. Despite being restrained he was in a gregarious mood, bellowing out renditions of *'God save the Queen'* whilst eyeing up the two young paramedics who stood tantalisingly close to him. They pretended to ignore him, as one might ignore a child who wanted too much attention, but he did not care. The prospect of a warm bed, hospital food, and the chance to ogle their shapely bottoms, had put a bit of lead in his pencil. So, he lay on the trolley without a care in the world, booming out the National Anthem with an enormous smile on his face. Finding a happy man who is being rushed to a psychiatric unit is not a common occurrence, but this tramp was far from common.

These trips had become Ground Hog days in their own right, with the modern-day Houdini invariably slipped free from his restraints and groped one of the paramedics. Barry Clark did not like the tramp one bit. He objected to his precious ambulance being vomited on and his beloved paramedics being harassed but had to accept that this was part of the job. Besides, they were only twenty minutes away from the hospital and it was nearly the end of his shift. So, he cast his opinions aside and jammed the accelerator to the floor.

As the ambulance drove through the winding Northumbrian B roads, the only sounds loud enough to be heard above the tramp's voice were the screams of the paramedics.

"For God sakes, will yoose put a sock in it, like! Ya canna sing," Britney implored in her broad Geordie accent. As she turned to look to her colleague Morag for support, the tramp saw his chance. In a flash, he had freed an arm and grabbed hold of one of Britney's shapely buttocks.

"Ya cheeky bastard," Britney screamed.

"Marvellous," the tramp slurred in a rich, Home Counties accent. "What a marvellous bottom you have, my dear. Top notch, I'll say."

"Piss off, ya perv," Britney shouted back as she pulled away from her troublesome patient.

Like a snake slithering its way out of a tangled mass of undergrowth, the tramp slipped loose from his bonds and staggered to his feet.

"Ah divn't know how ya do it," Britney continued, amazed that he had escaped yet again.

"Give us a kiss, my darling. Come on, just one little kiss for the road," he begged, as he stumbled towards her, wearing only the space blanket and an eager grin. The paramedics were not easily intimidated, but the smell of vomit and bits of half-digested carrot hanging from his shaggy beard were disconcerting to say the least. He moved exceptionally fast for a man of his age and blood alcohol level, and now with both arms free, he lunged at Britney, hoping to fondle her bosoms.

"Help, help us Barry, Jeez, get off us yah dirty," Britney shouted at the top of her voice, as she slapped the tramp with her open hand again and again. She was the prettier of the two paramedics, and therefore his prey of choice.

"Baaaaaaarrrrrrrry, do something," Morag screamed. "He's escaped and he's trying ta snog Britney, like. He's got puke all over his beard and he's getting real close."

Barry did not know what to do.

"Help, help us, Barry! Jeez, he's dizgoozting, like," Britney continued, but Barry was otherwise engaged. Past experience had taught him his best option was to get to the hospital as fast as he could. There was no reasoning with the grey-haired sex pest once he was in one of his frenzies, and if the nurses could hold him off for just a few more minutes they would all be okay.

"Give him some morphine, Morag," Barry shouted. His attention divided between the chaos in the back and keeping the ambulance on the road, as he took blind corners at seventy miles per hour.

"Ah can't. It's packed away in the box, and old pukey breath is in the way."

The temperature in the ambulance rose, the stress levels of the crew hit breaking point, the speedometer touched seventy-five, then eighty, and finally ninety miles per hour. Hedges and fences shot buy in a blur, as the engine strained, and a herd of cows in a nearby field bolted away from the noise. The old ambulance was not designed for such speeds, and at the same time less and less of Barry's attention was on the road. Then had a small but possibly relevant flicker of inspiration.

"What the hell," he thought, and balancing the steering wheel between his knees, Barry stretched his arms into the back, searching for any part of the tramp

he could get hold of.

Nothing.

"Damn it," he cursed, as his flailing arm found nothing but empty air. He was too late. The tramp had stumbled further down the ambulance, forcing the two nurses to the very back, and he was now well and truly out of reach. The ambulance ploughed on with Barry's foot not leaving the accelerator pedal, as he relied on divine intervention to keep them all from crashing. Britney's screams and the slurred rantings of the tramp did nothing to help Barry's concentration, and as they entered a hairpin bend a few miles south of Morpeth things looked like they could not get any worse...

o o o

"Enough umming," the lawyer snapped, and Barry fell silent. "I have further questions for you, Mr. Clark, and I would appreciate your undivided attention."

Barry nodded.

"When you finally staggered into Fenham Police Station you refused to give a urine sample. I am curious to know why?"

"Well, ah umm. Ah've got problems with me bladder, like. Ah'm a very sensitive person ya know, and if people force me to pee it's like, ah freeze, and ah joost can't go. You know what a mean?"

The lawyer raised an eyebrow.

"But you did eventually get over your shyness and give a urine sample, which confirmed the results of the breathalyser test, and put your blood alcohol level at over four times the legal limit."

"Yes, umm, ah realised they were not so happy with me refusing to urinate into their bottle, so ah asked for a bit of privacy and ah did. To be honest, it felt great, ah was dying for a pee, like."

The lawyer dealt with unintelligent people on a daily basis, but Barry's stupidity topped them all. The ambulance driver was so incompetent he did not need a prosecutor to come unstuck. He was more than capable of convicting himself.

"So, how do you explain this abnormally high reading when you had 'never tooched a drop, like'?"

Barry looked at his shoes.

"Ah, well, umm. There moost have been some kind of a mix up in the lab, or something. Ya know, with the results, like. It happens, ah've seen it on Casualty." Barry smiled, impressed with his own reply. The Lawyer smiled too; this case was winning itself.

"Mr. Clark," the lawyer spoke with a frightening calmness. "You seem prepared to tell us anything to get yourself off the hook. Do you honestly think we are convinced by your lies? Casualty is a fictional television programme, it's not real life. It is no more real than your fabricated stories of breathalysers and bladder complaints. I say you are a liar, and a liar who is going to pay for what he has done, and I will prove your dishonesty to the court in one final, indisputable way."

Barry gulped.

o o o

The ambulance continued to swerve all over the road, tyres screeching and rubber burning as Barry negotiated the deserted road. He had been driving ambulances since 1964 and had never crashed in all those years. When he first interviewed for a job with the Northumbrian Ambulance Service, he admitted he was an ex-alcoholic. The interviewers were impressed with his honesty, and despite some reservations, he got the job. It did not take long before Barry's lie was laid bare for all to see. His slurred messages on the intercom and the smell of beer wafting from his mouth at the start of his shifts were a giveaway. As fortune would have it, there was such a shortage of ambulance drivers that Barry's employers ignored his alcohol problem, put their heads in the sand, and hoped it would go away. It did not. Barry continued to drink as much, if not more than the tramp in the back of his ambulance, with the only difference being that Barry could hold the drink a little better. Now Barry's nemesis was pinning Britney against the side of the vehicle, his hands everywhere as he tried to give her a French kiss "*a la vomit*".

As the winding road became more perilous, the trio in the back bounced off the ambulance walls. Then, at a critical moment when the vile vagrant's hands were inches from Britney's panty line...

Thump!

The ambulance veered sharply to the left, shuddering violently as it collided with an object that was both heavy and large. Barry wrenched the steering wheel to the right, struggling to stay on the road. He should have pulled over to see what he had hit, but there was no way on God's good earth that he was going to stop now. He had to save Britney and Morag from the drunkard, who looked as though he was winning the battle for Britney's virtue.

Ernie's injuries would have healed a great deal faster had Barry stopped to help him, and Barry was not a man who would knowingly leave someone battered and alone by the roadside. After all, his job was to bring those who had been battered to hospital. He had his reasons for failing to stop at the scene of the accident. The first being the four Bloody Mary's he had polished off for breakfast. They had not helped his judgement at all. The second, was that he had no idea he had smashed into a young lad picking up a flower he hoped would bring him luck.

"Probably a sheep," thought Barry, and a dead sheep was collateral damage he was willing to accept. It all made sense in his foggy head. The sooner they got to the hospital, the sooner they would be free of the tramp, and the sooner they would get to the pub.

o o o

"Mr. Clark, you claim you took a break from work in order to walk your dog at the time of the accident. Is that correct?" The lawyer's question sent a shiver down Barry's spine.

"Erm yes, your Worship, that is correct. Molly, ma terrier, she's a wee beauty, like," Barry replied nervously.

"How long did you walk your 'wee beauty' for?" the lawyer continued, enjoying the chance to antagonise another soon to be criminal scumbag.

"About, umm, half an hour?"

"And where is Molly today?"

"Ah, umm, well."

The lawyer paused, making sure the courtroom could see that Barry was coming unstuck.

"Mr. Clark, I had two logistics experts look into your movements on the morning of the accident. They concluded that you would have needed to travel at just under the speed of sound to get home and walk wee Molly at the time you said you did."

"Oh," Barry replied, coming to terms with the fact that he had probably been rumbled.

"You see, I have written statements from several of your neighbours who claim you do not own a dog. Do you know what I think, Mr. Clark? I think you were as drunk as a skunk when you collided with poor Mr. Manning. I don't think breathalysers lie, but I think *you* do." The lawyer paused, inhaled deeply and continued. "Mr. Clark, you are a liar who should go to prison for being drunk whilst driving an ambulance, and then nearly killing an innocent teenager. A young man who was merely exercising his right as a human being to take a quiet walk in the countryside." The lawyer motioned to Ernie who was sitting in the public gallery making paper airplanes. Things were not looking good for the tipsy ambulance driver. Yet life has a funny way of doing exactly what it wants, and fate was about to intervene in Barry's life in a most peculiar way.

Debbie was a thirty-five-year old courtroom clerk with a magnetic smile, curvaceous body and a passionate zest for life. She had platinum blonde hair that tumbled over her shoulders like a mountain stream and had been a member of Mensa since she was twelve. Debbie was considered to be quite a catch in the law fraternity, but despite all the attention she received, she did not let her looks go to her head. She remained down to earth and generous, relying on her sharp mind and good old-fashioned hard work to make it in the legal world. That day Debbie was working as a courtroom clerk. However, she should not have been in that courtroom on that day because, by sheer co-incidence she happened to be Barry Clark's first cousin. She also happened to be dating the judge, who also happened to be married.

      The time that Debbie and the judge spent together, away from the dramas of the courtroom and the pestering of his fearsome wife, was priceless. To be lost in the arms of the vivacious courtroom clerk, laughing at her jokes and feeling thirty years younger was the highlight of his life, and the only reason he still turned up for work. He loved Debbie and had to hold himself back from blowing kisses to her from his chair in the courtroom. He did not know of her relationship to the defendant, but even if he had he would have kept him mouth firmly shut. The judge would do anything for his blue-eyed bombshell if she but only asked. In short, Debbie had the Lord Justice of Hexham wrapped tightly around her little finger and he loved every minute of it.

o o o

Seven minutes and eight torturous miles later, the ambulance screeched to a halt at the entrance of the Faraday Psychiatric Day Unit. Relative calm had been restored as twenty-five milligrams of morphine injected into the tramp's bottom, and thirty-four inches of leg thrust into his crown jewels took effect.

"Bloody chancer, like, trying ta snog us wi' puke all over his gob. Dizgoozting, man, bloody dizgoozting," Britney complained as she adjusted her tights and straightened her ruffled hair. "Ah tell yoose Morag, yoose was lucky ah stuck him one in the knackers. He went doon like a sack of spuds. Goodness knows what would've happened if ah hadn't saved us, like."

"Whatever Britney, yoose love the attention. You've got a thing fer older men, like." Morag joked. "You're probably gutted ah stepped in wi' the morphine. Yoose two were like Patrick Swayze and that bird in Dirty Dancing, like. Smooching away without a care in the world. Ha, ha, you little tart. If ah hadn't been here who knows what mischief yoose would be getting up to right now," the plumper nurse giggled as she teased her friend.

"Shoot yer face, Morag. Yer just jealous cos he fancied me, like."

"Away and shite yerself!" Morag laughed.

Meanwhile, the tramp did not seem to know when he was beaten. Despite being strapped to the trolley once again he was still trying to grab Morag's bum.

"Some people never give up, like. This guy is unbelievable," Morag gasped, subduing him with a choke hold.

A few second later two hospital porters arrived, and the still grinning tramp disappeared into the hospital.

"Thank God that's over," groaned Britney.

"Too right, we should get danger money for him, like," moaned Morag.

"Joost an hour more girls, and then we can gan get the beers in. Me mouths as dry as a badger's arse. First roonds on me," Barry declared, trying to distract himself from the splitting headache that was gnawing at his scalp.

"That's a first!" teased Morag. To which Barry slapped her on the bum.

"Ouch! Ya cheeky boogger," she yelped, then punched Barry playfully on the chest. "Ah should report yoose for sexual harassment, like."

"You'd be so lucky," Barry laughed, and hearing the walky-talky in the driver's cab squealing, he climbed back inside the ambulance to see if they had one final job to go to.

"Yes, yes, yes," he nodded as he took the emergency call. "Hexham. Okay. That's where we've joost come from. No problem. We'll be there," he told the operator. Wasting no time, Barry hung up and shouted to the two paramedics who were enjoying a cigarette break. "Come on girls, put those out, we've to go. There's some kid's been badly hurt, a hit and run, back in Hexham."

Morag and Britney threw their cigarettes to the ground, scrambled into the ambulance and slammed the rear doors shut. Barry shifted the old vehicle into first gear, revved the engine and shot off. His headache a thing of the past.

o o o

Debbie hated watching the lawyer picking Barry's flimsy defense to pieces. She knew she should not have been in that court room, but family loyalty was more important than a job. Barry had his problems, but he was a good man, and his Legal Aid defense lawyer was no match for the upstart from London. If there was any way she could help her cousin, she would. As the cross-examination went on, Debbie became increasingly agitated, but what could she do?

Finally, in the recess before the judge passed sentence, she saw her chance.

"That's it. Ah've had enough of this," she muttered, as she unfastened two of the buttons on her blouse, rustled her papers in an official looking manner, and marched over to the judge. After whispering a few well-chosen words in his ear, the judge's expression went from surprise, to delight, to concern, and finally to submission.

"*All I want is a quiet life*," he thought, and getting his ear chewed off by Debbie for sending her cousin to jail was not something he was willing to endure. His mind flashed to the possibility of Debbie leaving him and having to spend his spare time in the same room as his wife, perhaps even having to talk to her. That would just not do. So, despite the lawyer's clinical dismantling of Barry's story, the judge risked both his career and his reputation and let Barry off with a warning and an eighteen-month suspended sentence.

"I have decided to make an exception in Mr. Clark's case and let him keep his driving license," he told the stunned courtroom. "You see, the risk of him running someone over again is outweighed by the need to have someone to drive them to hospital if he did." The judge's argument made no sense, but he did not care, because Debbie was going to be happy. The lawyer glared at him and stormed out of the courtroom, furious. Not only had the lawyer lost an unlosable case, but his reputation had been tarnished and his fragile ego dented. Debbie, on the other hand was delighted, and decided to book herself and the judge in for a long weekend at a spa in Gretna Green. As the courtroom emptied, the judge and Debbie shot each other lustful looks, hoping no-one would notice, and a hung-over Barry returned to work the very next day.

o o o

It had not been a sheep that Barry had collided with. It had been a young man whose unconscious body lay motionless, hugging the trunk of a sycamore tree, a sprig of lucky heather clutched in his tiny hand. A trickle of blood ran from one of Ernie's nostrils as the most significant moments of his life flashed before him. Reliving these moments was almost as traumatic as the accident itself, because up until the collision his life had been one disaster after another. An image of himself as a thirteen-year-old, falling out of the bathroom window whilst squeezing a spot on his forehead, flashed before him. Then the face of the sweet old lady who had assaulted him with her umbrella, when he had tried to help her cross the road, breaking two of his teeth. The unfortunate incidents went on and on, and he would rather not have been reminded of any of them. Perhaps the lucky heather had some influence, because

Ernie was soon discovered by a local shepherd. The shepherd nearly drove his flock of sheep over Ernie's crumpled body but spotted him at the last moment and diverted them into a nearby field. Rushing up to Ernie, the shepherd could see he was too badly injured to move.

"Listen, lad," he whispered in Ernie's ear, unsure whether the boy could hear him or not. "Ah'm ganna call an ambulance. Ah'll be right back. Don't worry, ah'll make sure you're okay," then the kind-hearted mutton minder reassured him, then left his sheep and ran home.

o o o

"It's strange that there's been an accident on the very same road we just drove up. It must have just happened because ah didn't notice anything," Barry thought to himself as he sped towards Hexham. He drove in silence, focusing on the tarmac ahead of him, trying to remember if he had missed anything. Then the terrifying notion hit him. He remembered colliding with the sheep. *"What if it wasn't a sheep,"* he panicked. His blood stopped, his heart went cold, and his headache returned with a vengeance. The closer Barry got to the accident the surer he became. "*It must have been me. Ah was the one who ran over the boy.*" Barry's palms

were sweating. *"They never sweat,"* he told himself. His heart was now pounding, and he found it hard to breath. *"Oh, please God, let it not be me. Let there be a dead sheep somewhere along this road."*

As he turned a bend, he saw a shepherd standing in the road waving his arms above his head. His sheep were safely penned in the neighbouring field, and a figure lay by a sycamore tree at the side of the road. *"Oh shit, shit, shit, shit, shit. Please let him be alive,"* Barry prayed. Morag and Britney jumped out of the ambulance and rushed up to Ernie's body as Barry sat in the cab chewing his fingernails frantically.

As Morag and Britney put Ernie on a stretcher and carried him to the ambulance, they walked straight past a buckled license plate lying on the ground. The plate was hidden by the long grass, and had they seen it they would have known that the person responsible for this catastrophe was the very man who was going to drive them back to hospital; their friend and colleague Barry Clark.

"What kind of a scumbag would run over a kid and drive off, Barry? Ah mean, who hasn't got the balls to stop and call nine, nine, nine."

Barry did not say a word.

"It won't help anyway. Ah've got get this kid to hospital and put this whole thing behind me," he told himself, hating his every thought. The nurses got on

with stabilising their patient, giving him oxygen and keeping him alive as best they could. All the way to Newcastle Barry kept checking his mirror to see if the youngster had moved, willing Ernie to survive, trapped between guilt and hope. For the little man in the back, whose only wish had been to enjoy a quiet walk in the countryside, the day had not turned out too well. He had suffered a punctured lung, shattered pelvis and two broken legs, all of which put a bit of a dampener on his sixteenth birthday.

CHAPTER 2

Beauty and the Beast

The quiet hum of hospital machinery greeted Ernie as he woke. He had been broadsided by the ambulance four days before, and since that time had been lying unconscious in intensive care. Trying to open his swollen eyes he panicked, unable to escape the darkness.

"Ah'm blind, ah canna see, like. Ah'm blind!" he croaked, unaware that his eyes were caked in his own blood. As he lifted his head an inch off the hospital pillow a sharp pain shot through the back of his skull, compounding his fear.

"Ow!" he yelped as his head fell back onto his pillow.

A nurse hurried to his bedside.

"It's okay. You're safe, you're in hospital," she reassured him, laying a comforting palm on his forehead. "Don't struggle, you've had quite a knock. It's important you move as little as possible. At least for the next few days."

"Boot ah canna see. Help us. Please?" Ernie pleaded, unable to see the woman standing over him.

"It's alright. You're not blind. You're going to be able to see again. You've been in an accident, a serious one, and your eyes are swollen," she told him in a soothing voice. This was the hardest part of her job. The movies made it so profound when people awoke from comas, but the reality was quite different. They often had no idea what had happened, who they were, or what the hell was going on. "The swelling will go down over the next few days, and you should be able to see quite normally after that. We'll look after you, are you thirsty?"

"Yes, ah'm parched."

"Here, gently, take a sip of this," she told him, lifting a glass of water to his dry lips. The nurse's presence calmed Ernie, and he was able to swallow the lukewarm water from a plastic cup.

"Thank you," Ernie whispered.

"I can get you something for the pain, but you must try to relax. It will all make sense in a while. You've been unconscious for four days."

"Four days. How did ah get here? Ah don't remember anything, like," Ernie mumbled as he scoured the corners of his memory as best as his headache would allow. "Nothing," he whispered through blood-stained lips, "ah don't even remember me name."

"Your name is Ernie Manning; it was sewn into the collar of your jacket. You live in East Shields with your mum, Barbara. The police tracked her down, and she's been sitting right next to you since you arrived in intensive care. She popped out to get some fresh air, and then you came to. She'll be over the moon to see you've woken up." The nurse stroked Ernie's head kindly. In fifteen years of working in intensive care she had seen it all, but that did not make it any easier when a teenager got smashed up by a hit and run. "Don't worry about your memory either. It'll come back in good time."

The nurse was right, Ernie's memory did come back, well, most of it. He never recalled anything about the accident itself, and had the police not found a battered ambulance license plate at the scene, the cause of Ernie's injuries would have remained a mystery forever. The coppers put two and two together, and intercepted Barry just as he was walking into the Dog and Fox to continue his drinking binge. Barry was arrested and driven to the police station in handcuffs.

As he sobered up in an interview room, the police had informed Barry that the "sheep" he had hit was in fact a youth by the name of Ernie Manning. Mr. Manning had been seriously injured by Barry's ambulance, and to make matters worse, there had been a long delay in getting him to hospital as no other ambulance drivers could be found. A shameful Barry cringed with regret as he was charged with drink driving, dangerous driving and failing to stop at the scene of an accident.

o o o

Even the most eternal of eternal optimists would find it hard to describe Ernie as anything other than extraordinarily unlucky. The ambulance episode was only one in a long line of catastrophes that had blighted his short life. Had he been born a dog he would have spent his days cowering in veterinary waiting rooms with a lampshade fastened around his neck. Yet within the safe confines of the trauma recovery unit, his bad luck and innocent smile earned him plenty of sympathy from the staff. Three meals a day, *Monopoly*, *Risk* and *Cluedo*, and not a hint of danger was enough to guarantee that Ernie did not recover too quickly.

Over time he started to regain his strength, but the accident had ruined one of his knees, and his hips would never be the same again. The physios did their best but as the weeks went on it became clear that Ernie was never going to make a full recovery. Three months after colliding with the ambulance Ernie was discharged from hospital, facing the daunting prospect needing crutches for the rest of his life.

o o o

Ernie's childhood had been a lonely one. Lacking the confidence to make friends, he had spent most of his time in the company of himself. His classmates played football whilst the uncoordinated redhead sat on the sidelines, watching the other boys enjoying themselves, but never being allowed to join in. He longed to be part of the gang but whenever he tried to make friends it was a disaster, and he found himself on the wrong end of a good kicking. Ernie had lost count of the number of times he was admitted to casualty thanks to his classmates or one of the older boys picking on him. His mother did her best to protect her little angel, but that only made things worse. The cries of,

"Mummy's boy, Mummy's boy," rang in Ernie's ears for years. All Ernie wanted was to be accepted, but his unusual looks, gentle temperament and the nature of his mother's job ensured it never happened. Unable to trust people, he spent his spare time with animals. From a young age Ernie rescued injured birds or half-dead mice from the neighbour's cats, and then nursed them back to health. As he became a teenager, local people would deliver sick or stray animals to him, knowing the timid soul with the frown would take good care of them. Ernie did not know why, but he was really good at helping wild creatures, and was rarely without an animal or two nearby. Hamsters, gerbils, songbirds, rabbits, toads, hedgehogs and a rare African tortoise became the companions he had searched for in the human world. Only they were better than humans; safer, more predictable, and they never hurt him.

o o o

Ernie was born on the living room floor of a small, terraced house in the seaside town of East Shields in the autumn of 1968. Since the 1800's East Shields had been home to thousands of ship builders who scraped a living on the docks, at a time when the North East was building the largest and finest vessels in the world. Oh, how the mighty had fallen. By 1984 this small town had become a place of high unemployment and crime, full of young men who had little to do with their time. Some of these men were stereotypical 'Hard Northern Bastards'. They were as tough as nails and should have been grafting at the docks, but instead they spent their lives in smoke filled pubs and bookmakers. Bored and disillusioned, their frustration could boil over at any time, and they lived as if they were just waiting to tear some poor bugger's head off. Like most stereotypes, the term "Hard Northern Bastard" existed for good reason, and there were thousands of them all over Northumbria. Their presence terrified the mild mannered Ernie, who guessed the Vikings had a lot to answer for. Before the Vikings had turned up, their Celtic victims were by no means soft. However, the invaders who raped and pillaged the British coastline, added a certain 'Valkyrian' something to the Celts' gene pool, usually at the point of a sword. The pockets of beautiful blondes with an uncanny resistance to the cold and frighteningly short tempers, added weight to Ernie's theory. In East Shields, in the depths of winter, hordes of local women spilled out onto the streets at closing time; drinking, laughing and fighting, averse to wearing anything more than a boob tube, a mini skirt and high heels. It would be a foolish man who dismissed the connection between the bottle-wielding babes of Northumbria, and their slightly less intimidating ancestors in longboats, thought Ernie.

Ernie's upbringing had been far from conventional. He was the son of a welder? Roughneck? Fisherman? His mother was not sure, and this was not because his father had a particularly colourful CV. No, it was because Ernie's mum Babs was 'a lady of the night'.

Babs was a short, plump, attractive woman who had refused to let the world batter her down. Her life had been far from easy, but she had a glint in her eye and a wicked sense of humour. She and Ernie lived on the sea front, in a small, terraced house which looked identical to the hundreds of other houses built along the coastline. Their living room was small, the kitchen smaller and there were three tiny bedrooms at the back. One for Ernie, one for Babs, and the largest was reserved for business purposes. Babs was a homely woman with a natural warmth and a talent for listening. A kindly soul who made her clients feel loved. She had never planned to sell her body, but she had not had the choices that many people take for granted. Bringing up a child on her own in one of the poorest areas of the North East would have broken many people, but Babs was stronger than most.

Babs got no satisfaction from the physical side of her job, and she went through the motions on autopilot, whilst daydreaming about her next holiday or the last episode of Coronation Street. She saw it as her fate to deal with the loneliness of dysfunctional, middle-aged men, and it paid the bills. Besides, she had built up a list of clients who respected, and in some cases, loved her. Babs invariably greeted her clients with a kindly smile and a maternal hug, and then took them into her front room for an interview over a cup of tea and a Digestive biscuit. Having no desire to be bashed around like some of the other girls in East Shields, her "cup of tea interviews" became rites of passage, whereby her clients had to prove they were not thugs and knew how to treat a lady. If a man could be polite and considerate, dressed himself reasonably well, and kept himself clean, he was allowed into the bedroom. If not, he was turfed out of the door.

Babs saw herself as more than merely a body for men to have sex with. She cared about people and wanted to help them in any way she could. Her compassion was so obvious that some of her clients never made it to the bedroom and ended up pouring their hearts out on her couch. After years of having sex with strangers who told her far more about their personal lives than they should, Babs had become an accomplished counsellor. It never ceased to amaze her how lonely the average man was, and how hard they found it to express their feelings and dreams. Society had put a lid on the male occupants of England, and Babs was one of the rare people who gave them the space to be vulnerable. Unsurprisingly, most of her clients became fond of her, and as the years went on, she spent more time counselling and less time on the traditional side of the business. She liked it that way.

Babs made a good living and spent most of her money on her beloved Ernie. She adored her little boy, and spoiled him rotten, with clothes, bikes and fish suppers. He was the only man in her life who had ever bothered to hang around, and she saw only perfection in her shy, fearful, little son. For little Ernie, Babs was the most important person in the universe, and he put her on a pedestal so high she could have got lost in the clouds. Babs was the only person who had shown him love in a world where everyone else seemed out to get him, and the only person who made him feel safe. For a few years Ernie remained ignorant as to why so many men came and went from their home. However, Babs could not protect Ernie forever, and by the time he was eleven, he was all too aware of what was going on.

o o o

November 1985. The same day that Barry was getting a roasting from the lawyer in Newcastle, a rotund, hairless man in a suit was letting off some steam in London.

"Why the hell are you still here? Get out, you're

scaring the cockroaches," he spat from behind gritted teeth, hardly raising his voice, believing the venom it contained was more than enough to achieve his aim. "Now. Before I do something you'll regret." Nigel Kensington fiddled with the buttons on his silk shirt and did not bother to look at the young woman he was threatening. No, he was more interested in admiring his own reflection, as he stood in front of a magnificent, gold leafed mirror in the penthouse suite. In the background a panicking figure slipped in and out of view, scurrying here and there as she gathered her belongings. Picking up a dainty stiletto and then dropping it, as more of his callous words tore through her fragile frame. An empty bottle of *Veuve Clicquot* lay on the floor, with what was left of its contents soaked into the Persian rug. A broken mahogany chair lay wounded on its side, a single black lace stocking draped over its arm. She saw the stocking and darted towards it, quickly gathering it up.

She was physical perfection, even by the brutal standards of the international modelling industry. Tall, with chiseled features that had made her a fortune even though she was only nineteen. Her face had graced the front covers of both *Vogue* and *Cosmopolitan* more than once, and it was well known she had the fashion world at her feet. Every part of her priceless body was either trained, toned, manicured, plucked or otherwise pampered, and he had devoured it all the night before. This should have been enough to satisfy his wicked mind, but still he felt unfulfilled. This brute of a man reminded himself she was merely another in a long line of beauties who had failed to impress him. Why were they all so disappointing?

He, on the other hand, was almost as broad as he was tall, possessed a pudgy face that resembled a bulldog's bottom, and hard blue eyes that were as cold as the claws of death. At over six feet tall he cut an imposing figure. His head was shaven bald and deep craters covered his cheeks where angry spots had left their calling cards. Right now, *she* felt like the ugly one. The nobody. The less than nobody. So, she kept her head down, and hoped to escape her tormentor as quickly as she could. The whole scene was *Beauty and the Beast* gone horribly wrong, and he was enjoying every second of it.

"Why are you doing this to me?" she implored, craving an answer but fearful of what it might be. Her soft hazel eyes looked into his for a moment, and then she turned away, unable to hold his gaze. Rather than cutting her down further with more caustic words, he chose to ignore her, as she picked up the last of the clothes he had so tenderly stripped from her the night before. He had made her feel so special, so wanted, so much more than just the perfect body most men saw.

Nigel Kensington had wined and dined her in one of the most exclusive restaurants in London. The champagne had loosened their tongues, and they had laughed and joked about the fashion world, the mysteries of life and her grandmother's bunions. For years he had moved in the same celebrity circles she was learning to inhabit, and this created a bond of understanding between two people who had little contact with the everyday folk of the world. He had listened to her every word and exuded a charm so convincing she had stayed the night with him. He was also filthy rich, which did not hurt. In short, she thought she might have found the one.

"For God's sake, are you deaf as well as stupid? Get out of my sight. Get out," he snarled. "I don't want to hear any more of your whining." His educated accent cut deeper, because it had oozed such charm the night before.

"Ouch!" she yelped, as she stubbed her toe against one of the bed legs. A hint of a smile crossed his lips as she stumbled, clutching her injured foot. Hugging her belongings to her naked chest, the supermodel struggled to open the hotel room door. On the third attempt she worked the lock and squeezed through. How could any man be so kind and then so cruel? Hyde the seductive charlatan, had used Jekyll to get exactly what he wanted, and now Hyde had returned to torment her. Tears of frustration carried mascara down her cheeks, and only when she was safely out of the room did she stop and look back, as if to see for one last time if this monster was truly as cruel as he appeared.

"What did I do wrong?" she thought, hoping as young idealists do, that there was some good in this ogre, a part of him that could be nourished by the right woman. Perhaps by her?

Their eyes met. His expression told her she meant less than anything he had ever trodden on. Her expression told him he had won.

"Goodbye." he growled sarcastically.

She sobbed.

He snarled.

She left.

Satisfied he had caused so much hurt so early in the day, Nigel turned his fleshy face sideways and studied himself in the mirror. Noticing a spot on his forehead he squeezed it, wiped the pus away with a stubby finger, and cleaned the digit on the curtain next to him.

"Some say you're an ugly bastard Kensington, but the supermodels can't get enough of you," he told his reflection in a rich baritone that was filled with arrogance and pride. It took him no time to transition from ruining a young woman's self-confidence, to fawning over his own hideous image. Nigel was cruel to his core, and his cruelty was rarely hidden, except at those times when it served his own selfish purposes to hide it. Yet he was not just a bitter and twisted misogynist. He was far more than that. He was infamous. A man who spread fear, suffering and pain wherever he went. A man capable of overthrowing governments, collapsing economies, and destroying anyone who got in his way. In the murkiest and most powerful corners of the criminal underworld, Nigel Kensington was a man to be feared, perhaps *the* man to be feared, and that is why his real name was unknown to all but his closest employee. Nigel was instead referred to only by his alias. An alias that sent shudders down the crooked spines of criminals and politicians the world over. The fifty-eight-year old multi-billionaire, murderer, philanderer and criminal genius was better known as the Fat Man.

    The Fat Man pulled on his dark blue blazer, straightened his Ede and Ravenscroft tie, and buffed his Church's shoes against the bedclothes before leaving. As he marched through reception, an invisible force emanated from him that made people in the lobby look up from their newspapers and then quickly look down again. He left the hotel without paying or acknowledging the receptionists who looked nervously in his direction. The Fat Man was not remotely concerned about the bill or the state of his room. After all, there were another five hundred rooms in the hotel in Mayfair, and he happened to own them all.

o o o

"It's so unfair, Mam. Ah hate it, like," Ernie complained, as he slouched over the bowl of *Weetabix* he had spent the last quarter of an hour mashing to a pulp. On the kitchen sideboard stood a cage with an upturned glass water bottle strapped to its thin, metal bars. Inside, a brown rat with a make-shift splint on one of its hind legs hopped about gingerly. "That droonken ambulance driver ruined me life. Ah tried to do something good and nearly got me'self killed. He got hammered at loonch, smashed me legs to bits, and now he's back at work. It's not fair, Mam, and now ah'm stuck with these." Ernie's eyes welled up as he gestured to the pair of crutches resting against the kitchen table. Babs listened patiently, as her chubby fingers folded a Kevin Keegan special edition tea towel.

"Ah know Ernie. Life isn't fair, but perhaps some good will come of this? If it doesn't kill ya it makes ya stronger. Come on pet, enough feeling sorry for yer self, let's gan get some fresh air and blow the cobwebs away. It'll take your mind off it all."

"*Me mam's right,*" thought Ernie, relieved that

his mother was so wise.

"Alright Mam, as long as we don't go near any country roads. Ah've had enough of them to last me a lifetime," he joked. "Boot first, ah've got to feed Roland and check his leg. It's getting better every day."

"Oh Ernie, you're such a kind lad," Babs chuckled. "Always wanting to make the world a better place, eh?"

Ernie nodded, picked up one of his crutches, and hopped over to the cage to inspect the rat.

Babs and Ernie made their way to Cullercoats Bay, with Babs smiling proudly at her son.

"He's not the brightest bulb in the box, but he's a good boy, with a good heart, and what could be more important than that?" she mused, as they slowly walked along the Bay. *"If ah can get him through his teenage years there's every chance he'll have a happy life, and him being happy means everything to me,"* Babs thought, as she looked at the dark clouds gathering above them. Babs walked and Ernie hobbled up a gentle slope to the cliff tops at the end of the beach. The cliffs offered no shelter and the wind gusted fiercely, making it hard for them to hear each other. Babs and Ernie stood in silence for a while, appreciating the scenery and each other's company without the need for words. Ernie enjoyed being around his mother a great deal. Not only for the companionship they

shared, but also the wisdom she imparted. She did things deliberately, with a certain presence. Babs was a rock of stability in a time when most people were running around like headless chickens. She had been a safe haven for her catastrophic son since the day he was born and had kept him on the straight and narrow this far.

"This was a good idea, eh Pet? No point thinking about things when yoose can enjoy all this," Babs shouted over the wind as she gestured to the scene stretching before them.

"That's beautiful, Mam. Ah feel much better."

"Good. Ah hate ta see yoose sad. It's such a waste. Every day without laughter is a day wasted. You moost try to remember that, Ernie." Babs turned again to face the North Sea, taking in the splendour that stretched before her. She had always loved the vastness of the ocean. The way the white crests pawed at its dark grey surface, riding magnificently for a few brief seconds before being swallowed into its depths. In the distance, a solitary steamer cut through the strong currents, intent on delivering its cargo before finding its way home. Whenever Babs looked at the sea, she felt content, as all of her worries disappeared in an ocean of inner calm. "Ernie, can you take a picture of your old mam? Ah want something to remember this by," Babs shouted as she handed him her camera.

"Alreet Mam, but ah warn you, ah'm no expert with these things," Ernie shouted back as the rain began to pour down. Balancing on one of his crutches he fiddled with the camera, trying to fit the sea, the sky and his mother into the photograph. As he looked through the lens a faint feeling of happiness welled up inside him. His life was not so bad. The old dear loved him and he loved her, and as long as she was around he knew everything would be okay. He would not be alone, and his life would never go too far off track.

"Move back a wee bit, Mam," Ernie directed. "That's it, a wee bit more, that's grand, like."

"Is this far enough?" Babs asked, shuffling backwards, as Ernie squinted into the camera.

"A wee bit further, Mam."

"What about here? Is this okay?"

"Just a wee bit more, yes, a wee bit. That's grand."

A gust of wind nearly knocked Ernie of balance.

Click.
Slip.
Click.

Ernie took two photos before he noticed she had gone.

CHAPTER 3

Mirror, mirror on the wall

Standing a couple of feet in front of one of the many full-length mirrors in his Farringdon office, the Fat Man cast a formidable figure. A few days had passed since his unromantic liaison with the supermodel, and as usual he was dressed immaculately. However, despite his great fortune he felt glum. A black mood he could not shake off was consuming him, colouring everything he saw and thought. Looking closely at his reflection he glowered. Since the end of the summer he had put on more weight than he would have liked, and even the finest Savile Row tailors could not conceal this fact. For as long as he could remember, he had experienced success. Under his oppressive leadership his business had grown in both influence and wealth, and he was now the most powerful criminal to grace the shores of Great Britain. Some claimed he was the richest man in Europe, but because his wealth came from diabolically nefarious activities, *Forbes* would never publish this fact. The Fat Man would never be famous, but he had never wanted fame. Instead he lived a life far beyond that of the most famous people in the world.

Yet, something was not right. He had every material possession he could wish for but was plagued by a constant state of dissatisfaction. Having it all had not made him happy at all. Quite the opposite, his riches had taken the fun out of the simple pleasures he used to enjoy. Surely being able to do whatever he wanted whenever he wanted was the recipe to happiness? It seemed not.

"Why am I not happy?" he asked himself, demanding an answer from the mirror. He had always assumed he was, but perhaps he had just been busy? Perhaps he had thrown himself into the business so passionately he had never given himself time to reflect? He should be happy. He had everything he wanted; power, prestige, money, women, excitement. Yet these days they seemed to count for less and less. A good look at his associates would have told him that happiness and evil do not co-exist, but it never crossed his mind to look. His life had been about fulfilling *his* desires and to hell with everyone else. Was that wrong? Was there more to life than what he was experiencing?

For twenty-five years the Fat Man had believed his formidable achievements would bring him contentment, but the buzz of success did not last long these days. Sometimes he did not enjoy it at all. Or perhaps he no longer knew how to? Loosening his tie, he scowled as he forced a stubby finger under his collar.

"You haven't got any answers have you? Idiot!" he snarled. His dissatisfaction had become more pronounced since the summer. Something was stirring inside him and no matter how hard he tried to shake it off, it would not leave him alone. He could not help questioning all his ideas that had been set in stone. It was uncomfortable to suspect that his life's work had been a waste of time. He wanted to push this idea away, to forget about it, but trying to forget anything was the surest way to keep remembering it.

"Damn it," he shouted and smashed a flabby fist against the wall. It made no sense. *He* was the Fat Man. *He* could have whatever he wanted. Yet he felt so empty. Out of nowhere an old memory flashed into his mind. In his younger days he had been intrigued by the writings of a Tibetan monk whose name he had long forgotten. The monk had written at length about his experience of, "no mind", and claimed that both peace and true happiness came from this state. The monk believed that anyone could train themselves to find a space beyond thought and learn to live a life filled with contentment. All it took was a method, patience and consistency. All those years ago, peace and contentment had sounded rather tempting, and Nigel had considered travelling to the East to find the monk, but he had never got around to it. Greed and ambition had got the better of him, and the lure of peace had faded into the distance. That was when that traitor John Malone had betrayed him and set him on his evil path. The die was cast, and Nigel had become what he was today.

      All of a sudden, the Fat Man lost his balance and stumbled slightly. Perhaps it was stress or the devilled prawns, he was not sure. For a few seconds he became quite dizzy, and his image in the mirror appeared to morph into something quite different. Rather than a tired looking Fat Man in a bloated suit, he saw a slimmer version of himself dressed in saffron robes. He looked so young and serene sitting on a rock meditating in the mountains of Tibet or Nepal. There were fruit trees and narrow stone paths and songbirds singing all around him. One flew out of a nearby fruit tree and landed on his head, enjoying the company of a man who had mastered his mind.

"What the...?" the Fat Man gasped, and his reflection shimmered and returned to normal. He shook his head, as if to confirm the vision was nothing more than a trick of his mind. Taking a step closer to the glass he pressed his hand onto the mirror and a wave of sadness passed through him. He missed the life he never had.

o o o

Every time Ernie looked at the two photographs he had taken on the cliffs he cried. The first showed Babs standing on the cliff edge in front of a stormy sky, smiling proudly at her son. The second; a patch of grass, a stormy sky, but no Babs. In the blink of an eye Ernie's mother had slipped and fallen a hundred feet into the roaring waves below. She had perished without so much as a scream, thanks to her son, the unluckiest amateur photographer in the world.

Ernie's life fell apart. The one person who had ever cared about him was gone, and it was all his fault. He had killed his own mother. How could he ever forgive himself? There was no-one to talk to, no-one to have breakfast with, and no-one to keep his spirits up. He had not only lost his mother he had lost his best friend. No, he had lost his only friend. Ernie felt completely alone, and he was. He did not have any relatives to share his grief with, and although Roland the rat was alive and kicking, and had a cheerful disposition, he could not offer a great deal of emotional support.

The terraced house Ernie and Babs had shared felt empty, and his every waking moment was tormented by a guilt that overtook his young mind. Some of the teachers at school offered him counselling and the headmaster even gave him a hug, but Ernie did not want any of it. He believed he deserved to suffer for the terrible thing he had done, and he refused to take any help at all. Instead, he sunk deeper into himself, shutting out the world as best he could.

"Ah was right. The good times never last," he thought, over and over again.

o o o

Ernie feared he would never emerge from the talons of suffering that sunk into every part of his life. He woke in the morning feeling guilty, he ate breakfast and walked to school on autopilot, feeling guilty. He studied and learning nothing at school, feeling guilty. He returned home and distracted himself with television, but once the shows were over, the guilt returned. The thoughts crept up on him unaware. The suicidal ones. The hurtful ones. The ones that told him there was no point going on. He might have listened to them, had they continued for a few more weeks, but it was not time for Ernie Manning to leave the world. There were things he had to do, lessons to learn and people to love. He needed to play his part in the divine comedy of life even though it felt like a tragedy.

Two months after his mother's funeral something happened that turned Ernie's life around. A new girl arrived at Fountain High, and her name was Karen. Karen was a year older than Ernie, and the most beautiful creature he had ever seen. Every school day the smitten teenager hobbled to the front of the dinner queue, bought his lunch and found a seat in the canteen. There, Ernie would eat his ham and Philadelphia sandwich, sip at his carton of pasteurised milk, and watch Karen until the bell for afternoon lessons chimed. She was a goddess, an angel, the likes of which he had never seen before, and for those precious lunchtime minutes he felt alive again. He forgot his sorrow and his guilt vanished in a haze of teenage lust.

Karen was by anyone's standard a very attractive seventeen-year-old girl. She had a cheap perm, which bounced enticingly with every step she took, and wore a fake leather miniskirt which was shorter than most of the other girls' belts. Her skin-tight tracksuit top pushed her breasts into a cleavage that Ernie could have got lost in for days, and she chewed bubblegum as if she meant to destroy it, playing with it in the most erotic way imaginable. Her pale, muscular legs made Ernie's tummy feel funny, like when he used to climb the rope at gym class, and for many weeks he stroked and caressed those well-toned legs...

...In his dreams.

Ernie never forgot the first time he laid eyes on Karen, because she had had a run in with one of the older boys. The boy, one of the school bullies, made the mistake of pushing in front of her in the dinner line.
"Nice tits, can I..." he commented out of the side of his mouth, but before he could finish his sentence...

Crack.
"Ahhhhhhhhhhh."

Karen kicked him in the shins so hard, everyone in the canteen heard the scream and turned to see what was going on. The boy, who was a foot taller than Karen, started to hop on one leg clutching his shin. Without a second thought, she smacked him over the head with her metal dinner tray.

Crump.

"That'll show you for looking down my top you plonker," Karen told him calmly.

"Good on ya, girl," the dinner lady encouraged her, "and you," she turned to the boy, "piss off and don't come back until you've learned how to treat a lady. There's no food for you this lunchtime."

Ernie's love-struck eyes glazed over and he sighed with admiration. She was so commanding, so in control, so decisive and also calm. He was smitten, and from that moment forth, not a day went by when Ernie did not rush to the canteen to wait for Karen to join the queue. He could not take his eyes off this untouchable Siren, and although he had seen what happened to boys who looked down her top, he could not help himself. His mood started to lift, the guilt lost its tenacity, and he began feed himself on more than *Monster Munch* crisps and *Crunchies*.

Unlike the other girls at school who seemed so ordinary and mundane, Karen did not hail from the North East. No, she was far more exotic than that. She was more like a character out of that book Ernie had read in English, *The Lord of the Rings*. A gorgeous Elf with the pugilistic skills of an Orc, who had navigated her way into his pitiful life. A mysterious traveller from a distant and wonderful land.

o o o

An hour had passed and the Fat Man had not moved from his standoff with the mirror. Taking hold of one of his cheeks, he examined every part of it.

"Damn it!" There they were, for all to see, crow's feet. "I am getting old," and for a man as vain as him, the idea of aging was terrifying. He would soon be fifty-nine and his life of hedonism *had* taken its toll.

"Botox?" he wondered. *"No, injecting botulism into my face like some insecure pop star? Screw that,"* he shuddered. *"Perhaps it's time to find that Tibetan monk?"* That thought was nearly as terrifying as growing old. After everything he had done, he could never look a peaceful man in the eyes, and he knew it. His evil life had made him rich, but what price had he paid? The monk's words came back to him, echoing from a far-off place.

"Evil always brings about its undoing. Karma teaches us that what we give, returns to us."

Would all of the terrible things he had done come back to haunt him? The thought sent another shudder through his bloated frame.

"Karma? Bullshit," he muttered angrily, feeling more like an insecure pop star than he had ever done. He looked into the mirror once more. There was something else in the reflection staring back at him, something he had tried to ignore for months. There was something in his cold, blue eyes, almost…

A loneliness.

Pushing this thought to the back of his mind he insisted,
"I am not lonely. How could I possibly be lonely? I can be with whoever I want, whenever I want," but his words sounded hollow. Who was he trying to kid? He was beginning to learn that nothing lasts forever, and his mortality was catching up with him. Was this the start of a midlife crisis? Or was he already well and truly submerged in one? The Fat Man was quite brilliant at playing the role of ruthless boss, but he knew he was losing his taste for violence. He could force it, he could fake it, but it was becoming more distasteful to him by the day.

"Am I going soft?" It was not something he thought would ever happen. He did what he could to keep himself sharp, on the edge. Yet, perhaps life had its own wily ways of softening the hardest of hearts? Perhaps he was becoming weak? It would only be a matter of time before people noticed this weakness, and then he would be in trouble. "Retirement. At least for a while. It has to be," he told himself firmly, not daring to look in the mirror for fear the saffron robed image would return. Retirement was something he had planned for. A necessity which lay hidden in the background, in case the heat got too much, and he had to disappear. Yet now he was faced with the possibility of leaving the business by choice, not necessity, and that was a different matter. Staring at the mirror for what seemed like minutes, his mind raced from option to option. The idea of being a nobody was painful for a man whose whole life had been built by his cruel and inflated ego. Could he live with himself if he had to let go of all of his power? It was not tempting. Would he be any better than a broken factory worker weeping at his retirement. Knowing he will be replaced by a younger man who can do his job faster and better? Once the Fat Man was out of the picture, others would fight for a piece of the pie. His vacuum would be filled and he would be nothing more than a distant memory, a story told by drunken cons in East End pubs. Could he live with that?

"I'll bloody well have to," he scowled. With this thought and with the ease of someone used to making life or death decisions on the role of a dice, it was decided. As soon as he could he would be kicking back on his forty-thousand-acre estate in Cordoba, Argentina. Free from the irritation of extradition treaties, in the company of other associates who were enjoying a crime funded retirement there. It would be a safe and luxurious place to enjoy the rest of his life, and he was certain he could keep himself entertained.

However, he must stop his wicked empire going to the dogs. There had to be a way around giving up his ill-gotten gains to the pathetic criminals who would step into his vacuum. He had considered handing it all over to the boy, but since he was born his son had been such a disappointment. He possessed so few of his father's qualities the Fat Man wondered if there had been a mix up at the hospital, because of this the Fat Man had never included his son in the business. Yet despite his misgivings, the boy was his own blood and might improve with age and less than tender nurturing. He also had one significant advantage over the other candidates. He was the only one. The Fat Man did not have any other children that he knew of, and he had killed off any employees who were ambitious enough to be a threat. That ambition had been dangerous in the past, but now it was exactly what he needed. None of the monkeys he currently hired could be trusted with such an awesome task. No, the boy was a little soft around the edges, but he had potential.

The Fat Man took a moment to gather his thoughts. Had the monk-like image in the mirror been his imagination? Or the life he could have had if he had made different choices? He knew the answer but did not want to admit it to himself. What he did know was that peace and happiness would have to wait for a while. He had to bring the boy up to speed. One way or another he was going to leave his empire with a leader fit to lead it, and then perhaps he could look into his more sentimental desires. As was so often the case when the Fat Man stopped thinking about a problem and made a decision, his mood lifted. His mind was not happy, but at least it was now occupied with possibilities. His new mission had given him some sort of purpose and made it all too easy to cast aside his desire for peace.

o o o

Karen Walsh came from Huntstapleton, a humble seaside town nestled unassumingly in the Norfolk coastline. In the 1980's Huntstapleton was a summertime resort for simple folk with modest means who shied away from anything too exotic, but to Karen it was home. Karen had never met her father and her mother had passed away when she was only thirteen. That was when her mother's sister, Rose, had taken on the responsibility for bringing Karen up. Rose had always a soft spot for the rebellious teenager and treated Karen as her own. Life with a teenager in mourning was not all smooth sailing, and Karen's wild side that got wilder after her mother's death. She stole cigarettes from the corner shop and fought with the boys at school, but Rose continued to see the good in her niece, hoping she would come to terms with her demons and find some semblance of peace.

Huntstapleton had a way of sucking people in, and Karen and her Aunt would probably have stayed there for the rest of their lives, had it not been for a series of bizarre events which unfolded that summer.

Every June thousands of lager swilling bikers descended on "Sunny Hunny." These larger-than-life lumbering walruses hung out in the greasy cafes, or sunbathed on the pebbled beaches, fully dressed in black leathers with their Harleys parked close by. The smell of beer, cigarettes and wacky-backy hung around them, but for the most part they were a friendly bunch. There was something to be said for the freedom of a motorbike, a gang of good friends, and the ability to make the most out of what little they had, and these bikers did that with aplomb. The council invested a great deal of time and money catering for their eccentric guests, who doubled the income of the small town. Pictures of Huntstapleton were displayed on billboards at Superbike events all over the country, extra rubbish bins and bright green portaloos were shipped in, to make life a little more luxurious for their two-wheeled guests. Although Portaloos are not generally synonymous with beauty, when fifty of them were lined up side-by-side on Huntstapleton's shoreline, they looked quite breathtaking, like a sea of radiant, portaloo green.

As any half-decent Gastroenterologist will testify, many years spent devouring tons of red meat and drinking gallons of beer can put a strain on the bowels. The relief these simple plastic structures offered to the overindulgent bikers was hard for mere mortals to comprehend. It was not only functionality they provided, but entertainment value too. The less sophisticated bikers took great delight in tipping them over whenever one of their friends was about to deliver his offering to the gods. Thus leaving him trapped inside until someone was kind enough to tip the portaloo back to its original position and let him out. This ritual went on for years without any casualties, bar the occasional broken nose as a furious victim dealt out his stinking revenge. That was until Hefty Harry, a well-known biker, whose nickname failed to differentiate him from any of his peers, came a cropper.

There were two things that Hefty Harry loved. The first was his *Harley Davidson*, and the second was ramming as many greasy burgers into his overloaded digestive system as he could. A notorious prankster, Hefty Harry had been due some payback for a long time, and today was the day he was going to get it. It was a scorching June afternoon when Harry lowered his ample buttocks onto the Portaloo seat, a *Benson and Hedges* in his gob and the *Daily Mirror* clasped in his oily fingers. Settling down for a good long read, he was unaware that three of his friends had crept up behind his portaloo. The mischievous trio grinned at one another, and taking a firm grip they whispered,

"One, two, three, over we go." The three bikers giggled as they heaved the toilet onto its front.

"Holy shit!" screamed Hefty Harry appropriately. His broken cigarette burning his cheek as he lurched forward and crashed head first into the loo door.

Smack.

His friends collapsed in fits of hysterics, congratulating themselves on a feat of comic genius that would have made Bobby Davro proud. As the bikers rolled around on the grass giggling, Harry, who had broken his neck, gasped his last breath.

The whole biker community was shaken to the core by the news of Harry's death. A week later Harry's hefty coffin was driven around the streets of Huntstapleton, accompanied by a mass of mourning bikers in full ceremonial dress. Accompanied by over four hundred leather-clad souls, Zippo lighters held aloft, the well-liked joker was lowered into a grave and buried with a little help from a JCB digger and a crane.

The local minister gave a touching eulogy for the man who had made so many people laugh, and most of the bikers saw Harry's death as a tragic accident, a practical joke gone wrong. However, a few believed it was nothing short of cold-blooded murder. The previously peaceful motorcycle gang fractured, and all hell broke loose. Former friends took up arms against each other, and the streets of the previously peaceful town were no longer safe for law-abiding citizens. In pitched battles that rivalled Spartacus in their ferocity, there followed three serious assaults, a spate of vandalism and an armed robbery. Unrest such as this was unheard of in Huntstapleton and led to the formation of the Norfolk police's first rapid armed response unit. This came as a shock to the law-abiding citizens of the quiet town, who were used to having policemen and women whose most glamorous tasks were investigating the odd burglary and kicking the locals out at closing time. The tabloids had a field day.

"Psycho Biker Death War."
"Biker Yobs in Six Week Killing Spree."
"String 'em Up! Barmy Bikers Cause Mayhem in Sunny Hunny."

They declared without regard for the damage

their fearful headlines might do. It was terrifying for Aunt Rose, who decided the streets of Huntstapleton were no longer safe for a teenaged girl. Particularly a girl who took a bit too much interest in the bikers and their escapades. After a trip to Tesco's, where Karen was wolf-whistled and responded by blowing a Marylyn Monroe style kiss back at the biker, Rose knew enough was enough. She got home, called up an estate agent and rented number twelve Acacia Avenue in a small town near Newcastle called East Shields. She and Karen packed their belongings and moved north, where Rose hoped to start a new life away from the troubles they had left behind.

Treating East Shields as a haven from danger was not unlike moving to Syria to get a bit of peace and quiet, but Aunt Rose knew nothing of this.

The usual worries and insecurities of starting at a new school did not phase Karen at all. She had an old head on her shoulders and a healthy cynicism, which gave her an aura of cool that most people were wary of. As the new girl in year eleven with a strange accent and a pair of bright pink Doctor Marten boots, Karen qualified to be picked on. That was just fine with her, because she loved a good dust up, and like most people who enjoy fighting, she was rather good at it. By the end of Karen's first week she had put three of the biggest boys in year six out of action and scared the hell out of a few of the teachers. Karen was no wilting violet, and Ernie could not help falling head over heels in love with her.

"She's totally out of your league, man. Look at you, you're a cripple. You can't even walk without crutches," one of his classmates scoffed as the love-struck Geordie sat in his usual chair watching Karen tucking into a plate of cod and chips. Ernie did not reply, but he had to admit it, the kid was right.

"She is totally outa ma league. Besides, ah haven't got the guts to talk to her anyway." Ernie knew he lacked the confidence and looks to impress such a babe. He was one of life's losers and that was just the way it was.

CHAPTER 4

Half wit

The Fat Man skidded his Aston Martin to a halt in an industrial area on the outskirts of east London. The desolate brick walls of the warehouse were a distant cry from the luxury of the Fat Man's penthouse suite. His previous night's liaison with the supermodel had been a passable distraction, but it was nothing compared to the satisfaction of removing certain irritating "obstacles" that had been in his way. Struggling to pull himself out of his quarter of a million pound sports car he then strode across the grim, grey car park heading towards the House of Horrors.

"Morning Mickey," he nodded to the bald-headed bouncer on the door, then trotted down a pitch-black staircase and disappeared into the derelict building.

"Get a move on lads, we haven't got all day," the Fat Man barked at two men in bloody overalls who had just finished dismembering a body. "And Spider, let me count those limbs, I don't want anything left that could cause us any problems."

"Sure boss," the thin man answered in a quiet, deliberate almost sinister lilt. Of all the Fat Man's hired thugs Spider was the most peculiar and the most feared. He was nearing fifty yet had had train-track braces for as long as anyone could remember. His jet-black hair was combed into a greasy side parting, and a small moustache that was perched right under his slightly pointed nose, made him look unnervingly like Adolf Hitler. No one had a clue if Spider was emulating the dead Fuhrer, or if he just had a terrible sense of fashion, but no-one except for the Fat Man had ever dared to ask. Quite why he had earned the nickname "Spider" no-one knew, but his heart was as cold and ruthless as the most deadly of arachnids.

Spider stacked body parts into a pile on the hard cement floor, before packing them into bin liners and securing them with duct tape. The Fat Man didn't visit the House of Horrors very often. It was a risk he didn't like to take, but from time to time he would pop in, just to keep Spider and the boys on their toes. He was a firm believer in leading by example and would have done some of the dismembering himself, if he hadn't been wearing a five-thousand-pound suit.

"One, two, three, four, five, six, seven," the Fat Man counted seven right arms, and, "one, two, three, four, five, six… Only six left arms! Spider, what the hell?" he shouted, "There's only six left arms."

"No worries boss," his employee hissed without looking up, "I slotted One Armed Jack, remember?"

"Oh, yes. Good." The Fat Man relaxed. Picking up an arm that was lying next to him, he examined it as if it was a piece of steak, and then eased a gold ring off one of the fingers. Wiping the blood off with a rag, he put the ring in his mouth and bit down on the metal to test its quality. "Nice little souvenir," the Fat Man grunted, then put it in his pocket and went inside to eat breakfast.

o o o

The following day the Fat Man squeezed through the glass double doors that led out of his office and was instantly immersed in the hustle and bustle of the City of London. Newspaper vendors shouted at passers-by in a language that bore no resemblance to English. Queues of stationary cars pumped out greenhouse gases as their frustrated drivers tooted their horns, and a happy face was nowhere to be seen.

The Fat Man marched down the street, passing a sea of lifeless souls, united by eerie, white complexions and furrowed brows, suited men and women who walked at double speed. Their resigned expressions revealling the hellishly long hours they spent behind a desk every week. These tragic beings earned more in a month than most people earned in a year, yet their money had not bought them a semblance of happiness. They had the fast car and the huge house but were empty of purpose or meaning. The barren moral ground from which they had chosen their careers, had swallowed them up whole, leaving jittery, high-strung wrecks where youthful promise had once been. These robots rarely looked up from the pavement, for fear they may catch someone's eye and be forced to make contact with another equally miserable human being.

One of the Fat Man's greatest pleasures was provided by the charity workers who made a living persuading members of the public to sign away ten pounds a month to one deserving cause or another. He revelled in the fear they instilled in the office workers who shared the same pavements. The office workers would almost unanimously react with alarm whenever the charity workers approached, but he did not. Unlike his fellow pedestrians the Fat Man relished his encounters with the charity workers, in the same way a lioness relishes an encounter with a wounded wildebeest calf. They were deluded idealists, he thought, and it was his job to educate them in the harsh ways of the world.

Today a scruffy, dread locked man caught his eye. Catching the Fat Man's eye was easy, as he made a habit of staring down anyone who dared wander into his gaze. He guessed the man was about nineteen, and most probably a gap year student. He was wearing an oversized bright orange T-shirt which hung from what the Fat Man assumed was an unwashed body.

"Would you like to help disabled people, sir?" asked the charity worker, trying to disguise his hangover with a forced smile. He was from Sydney, travelling the world for a couple of years, seeing the sites and having as many adventures as he could afford. Every few months his cash would run out and he would work for a while. Collecting for charities was better paid than fruit picking, but it was not easy to prize money out of the richest people in London.

"Of course. Who exactly are we helping?" The Fat Man's threatening grin revealing a row of perfectly white teeth. His huge frame cast a shadow over the Australian, and his icy blue eyes bored into him. The charity worker did not notice how evil the man standing in front of him was. Had he been more alert, he might have smelled it and walked away. Instead, he lit up at the Fat Man's enthusiasm to the question he asked hundreds of times each day. "Hmm. Helper Care," the Fat Man continued, pointing at the charity worker's T-shirt, "If I'm not mistaken that's a charity for the physically disabled?" His tone was unassuming, feigning both ignorance and interest at the same time. That was the best way to suck them in, pretending he actually cared.

"Yes, we have over two hundred employees in the UK and over..." The drivel had started. The Fat Man listened for a minute, tapping his foot impatiently, and then cut the charity worker short.

"I assume you are collecting money to force these lazy scroungers to do some kind of work?"

"Wh... what did you say?" the charity worker stammered.

"Deaf, as well as stupid, I see. It's a well-known fact that most disabled people aren't really disabled, they're just bone idle."

"I, I'm sorry. Did I hear you right?" the Australian asked, aghast, a look of horror on his face. All of a sudden he felt like a minnow who had been separated from its shoal and was about to be devoured by a hungry barracuda.

"I'm surprised you can hear anything with all that shit clogging your ears. You know in this country it's common courtesy to take a shower now and again?" the Fat Man sneared.

"You think these people want live off donations? Is that what you mean?"

"I merely asked if you were collecting moneys to get these people off their backsides, and into gainful employment? Is that so difficult to understand? Perhaps you've inherited too many mentally ill genes from your ancestors? You are from Australia, are you not?"

How dare he? Every day the charity worker tried to not be affected by the many rejections he endured. People ignored him, some scowled at him, others ran in the opposite direction, but no-one had ever said anything like this before. A fountain of indignation bubbled up inside him.

"How could anyone be so cold-hearted?" He so wanted to come back at this monster with a reply that would take him down a peg or two, but could only manage,

"Well, screw you. Just because you don't care, doesn't mean other people don't. Be like that." Psyching himself up he added, "you fat, heartless bastard."

"Overweight, perhaps, but I have made more money wasting my time talking to you than you will earn in ten years," the Fat Man replied. The horrified charity worker fought to stop himself bursting into tears on the pavement. That would have given this brute too much satisfaction. Besides, being lost for words was frustrating enough. No doubt he would think up a brilliant response five minutes later, after this arsehole had gone.

"Perhaps ten minutes," the Fat Man thought as he read the Australian like an open book, *"he looks a little slow."* The Fat Man's crocodile grin broadened as he took out a crisp fifty-pound note from his bulging money clip, tore it into pieces and blew it all over the pavement.

"There you go, something for your time. Oh, and one more thing, I wasn't joking about the shower, I can smell you from here. Goodbye." Then the Fat Man barged past the Australian and marched away, while the shell-shocked youngster knelt on the pavement gathering up the pieces of the desecrated note.

o o o

The Fat Man had his fingers in a lot of pies, but he had made most of his money in property. Property ownership, property arson and property protection rackets had made him into a multi-millionaire by the time he was thirty. However, his first million had come via the stock market at the tender age of twenty-five. Now, over thirty years later, he no longer needed the money, but still dabbled in the stock market to while away the boredom of billionairedom.

His latest deal involved him stumbling across information volunteered by a man who was being dangled from the Clifton Suspension Bridge. The unfortunate businessman was an executive director of Trasco, a pharmaceutical company specialising in developing drugs to treat Alzheimer's. The director was thoroughly corrupt and had co-operated with a rival criminal network for much of his career. The heavy holding the director's legs was the Fat Man's most trusted employee, Mickey 'the Bouncer'. The trembling director revealed that Trasco was days from announcing it had discovered a drug that could delay the progression of the disease. Big news in the pharmaceutical world. News that could change the lives of a generation. Once the director had spilled his guts about the new drug the Bouncer let him go.

The stock market does not like it, when director's jump off bridges and Trasco's share price took a dive. That was when the Fat Man bought twenty eight percent of the company on the cheap, through a number of shell trading companies he controlled. Two weeks later the news of the Alzheimer's breakthrough was made official, and Trasco's shares shot up over six hundred percent. The Fat Man sold his shares, having made over fifty million pounds profit for half a day's work that he did not even do.

Striding towards his office in Smithfield, the Fat Man barged his way through a gaggle of foreign students, booting a black Labrador in the ribs as he went. The fact that the dog was attached to a blind person was an added bonus. The Fat Man did not do anything by half. He had a band of industrial spies, ex-cons and money hungry investment bankers on his payroll. Between fifty and a hundred criminals, depending on who was being useful, and who had outlived their usefulness. Looking at his Patek Philippe wristwatch, he decided he still had a little time before he needed to get back to work. So, he zeroed in on another charity worker standing on pavement just ahead of him. Licking his lips, he moved in for the kill, he had just enough time for one more before dinner.

o o o

Tarquin sat hunched at his desk, a sweaty palm supporting his chin, as he surveyed a VDU inches from his face. His palms were too clammy to be healthy, but he did not notice. He was too caught up in his thoughts to notice anything other than the mass of figures blinking away at him. Two computer screens stood on the desk in front of him, with hundreds of prices flashing and changing every second. He was in the heart of a top investment bank somewhere in the belly of London, his eyes were sunk into dark sockets, his body stiff, and he had far too many wrinkles. Tarquin was in his mid-twenties, but he felt an awful lot older, and as he looked around the office everyone else looked too old too.

It was eight o'clock in the morning and he had been in the office for two hours, thinking about how much he hated his job. Thinking like that hurt. He had been in Paris that weekend with Zoe. It should have been magical, but it was so hard to relax. On his desk lay two heavy, plastic phones, one for each ear. Their tangled chords reminding him of Friday's final trade. A trade where he had screamed at a client whose heart had been sealed shut with molten lead.

"Why did I ever get into this business," Tarquin thought. *"Oh, yes, the money,"* he sighed. *"Fuck the money."*

He knew there must be more to life than this, but he was damned if he knew what it was. His father was rich, his grandfather had been rich, so Tarquin had decided he had to be rich. The price his body and mind were paying for this decision was beyond a joke. He did not even enjoy the good things anymore. Eating out; he thought about work. Skiing in Verbier; he thought about work. Making love to Zoe; well, no thoughts of work, but as soon as it was over. Work. Tarquin was earning a six-figure salary, but did that make him happy? It certainly paid for him to be miserable in exotic locations, but happiness had drifted from his grasp too long ago for him to remember. Most of the time Tarquin felt like he was existing, and certainly not close to truly living.

"What am I doing here?" He wondered, day after day. Yet still he drove himself on. Still he turned up for work, an unseen force pushing him to sell his soul as a Trader in one of the hottest financial cauldrons on earth. He was right in the centre of the City of London, the Mecca of the financial world. A risky, lively place, where fortunes could be made or lost in minutes, yet he was bored. *"Keep going. Just keep your head down, only a few more years."* He told himself. Perhaps it was ambition? Perhaps it was fear? Perhaps he just had no idea how else he could make so much money? Tarquin was chasing the dream but forgetting to enjoy life along the way. A young man who felt like an old man, aching with a boredom that filled his so-called 'successful' life. He was sure there must be another way to earn the big bucks. He had to find a way out.

o o o

Nipping off for a sly cigarette as an alternative to double maths was one of Karen's favourite pastimes. No matter how hard she tried, she could not figure out why she had to spend hours of her valuable time learning something she could do with a simple calculator. However, right now she was more interested in having a cigarette than trying to reform the British education system. The other smokers went behind the bike sheds, so Karen did not expect to bump into anyone behind the English block, and she liked it that way. She relished this time on her own, away from the idiots at school. She had been at Cullercoats High for a month, but the pretty brunette had not made any friends. Deep down she would have liked to have one or two pals to hang out with, but convinced herself that she was fine being the loner.

"Life's easier when you only have to look out for yourself, and let's face it, people only let you down," she thought, as she sucked on the comforting filter of a *Silk Cut*. Besides, the sweet taste of tobacco was all the more enjoyable when she did not have anyone to distract her with idle chit chat.

Thump.

A noise interrupted Karen's first drag.

Thump.

There it was again.

Thump.

Stubbing out her cigarette, Karen calmly popped a Juicy Fruit into her mouth and walked around the back of the English block to see what was making the noise. The sight that met her filled her with rage.

o o o

Rolling on the ground in front of Karen, covered in mud was the skinny, but kind of cute redhead she had noticed staring at her in the dinner queue. He was curled up in a ball, his eyes tightly closed, whilst an older boy was kicking him in the ribs for fun.

"Loser. Loser. Loser," mocked the older boy, who must have been twice the size of the little guy on the ground. The redhead said nothing, although he grunted in pain every time the bully connected with a kick to his ribs. The expression of anguish on his face, as he prayed for the beating to stop, was more than enough to fire Karen into action. She moved like a whirlwind.

Smash.
Crack.
Yelp.

Karen punched the bully hard on his nose, then kicked him in the shin and followed with a knee to his groin. It was all over in less than five seconds. The bully fell to his knees clutching his wounded snout, and tried to curl himself into a ball, but Karen grabbed his hair and forced him to look her in the eyes.

"Picking on a little guy with crutches. What kind of a tosser are you? Haven't you got anything better to do than hurting people?"

"Ow, ow. Ah'm sorry, Ah'm sorry. Please, no more pain," the bully squealed, having never faced so brutal an adversary.

"Did you not get enough hugs when you were little? Or maybe you got too many? Lucky for you I'm in a good mood, but next time, I won't be so nice," she warned. Satisfied he had learned his lesson, Karen let go of his hair and the shocked bully scrambled to his feet, limping off as fast as his trembling legs would carry him.

Ernie waited, and then slowly uncurled himself like an armadillo, still wary the bully might return. His face was caked in mud, and blood flowed from a gash on his chin, staining his Newcastle United football top a rich vermillion. He dare not look at the girl who had saved him, but as their eyes eventually met he quickly forgot the pain. Here he was, kneeling at the feet of the most beautiful woman he had ever laid eyes upon. The goddess from the dinner queue, whom he had watched from afar and dreamed about at night, had rescued him. His mouth went dry, his heart pounded, he was dumbstruck. Ernie wanted to say, 'thank you', but although he mouthed the words, nothing came out. Karen too, felt strangely out of control, and as she offered a hand to the scruffy redhead she could do nothing other than smile. After a lingering moment of awkward silence she regained her composure.

"You're the boy who stares at me in the dinner queue," she said a little threateningly, as she picked up one of Ernie's crutches and helped him to his feet. His little hand was soft, and his touch quite delightful.

"Please don't hit us, like," Ernie stuttered in a shy, apologetic voice. "Ah didn't mean anything by it," he added, cowering from the girl he admired and feared more than anyone.

"I won't. Look at you, you've got blood all over your top," Karen said, taking out a tissue and dabbing his chest.

"Ah'm Ernie by the way."

"K.. Karen," she blushed.

"Thank you for helping us."

"Why did he hurt you?" Karen asked.

"He was plucking the legs off a family of flies, and ah told him to stop. Stupid eh? Look what happened. Ah should've kept me mouth shut, like."

"No. No way. You did the right thing," Karen insisted, trying to hide her embarrassment. She never felt like this with guys. There was something so innocent about her new friend. It felt so natural to stand there and talk to him.

"Ah don't mean anything by staring at you at lunch, like. Ah just, it's just, well, you are so," he gulped, "so, beautiful."

In seventeen years, no-one except Aunt Rose had told Karen she was beautiful, and her heart, which she had kept tightly shut for as long as she could remember, fluttered opened a little. That day in the mud behind the English block, fate conspired to bring two most unlikely people together. Two youngsters, who had no idea of it at the time, but had been destined to find each other, and embark on a journey that would take them to the happiest and the darkest of places. They both felt it, neither understood it, but from that day on Karen Walsh and Ernie Manning were inseparable.

o o o

Tarquin sat in the passenger seat of the dark green Aston Martin DB7, with the sweaty figure of the Fat Man sitting beside him, muttering something to himself. The Aston was travelling as fast as the blood was draining from Tarquin's face, as the driver pushed it as hard as he possibly could. It had been a week since the Fat Man's unromantic liaison with the super model, and he had decided to take young Tarquin for a drive, but as usual Nigel's near permanent state of aggression was getting the better of him. First the stress of the trading floor, and now this. Tarquin really wanted him to calm down. As if Tarquin's prayer was being answered, the Fat Man pressed play on his compact disk player. Tarquin hoped the track would do the trick.

"Money, money, money…"

"Bingo!" thought Tarquin, as *Abba* boomed out of the two speakers in the back. The Fat Man's lips hinted a smile as his favourite Scandinavians cranked it up. The DB7 slowed a little, but Tarquin's rest bite did not last for long.

"So tell me Tarquin, how rich do you want to be by the time you're thirty-five?" the Fat Man asked his terrified companion, as he took a blind corner on the wrong side of the road at eighty-five miles per hour. *Abba* or no *Abba*, charging through the back roads of Surrey was the Fat Man's preferred way to conduct business, particularly with those he wanted to intimidate. It kept small talk to a minimum.

Both men wore the best tailored suits money could buy, and sported haircuts which cost about the same as a night in one of the Fat Man's hotels. The Fat Man insisted on going to London's top hair salon for a head shave every week, even though he could have done the job himself in minutes. Tarquin was good looking in a boyish sort of way, and like the driver he spoke with an upper-class English accent. Although his words came out a little faster than the maniac behind the wheel. Unlike the Fat Man he was slim and small boned, with a short back and sides, and a fringe that flopped over his face whenever the Fat Man braked.

"*Oh no,*" Tarquin thought, suspecting whatever answer he gave would be the wrong one. He was usually so silver tongued, so slick with his words he could tie anyone in knots. For Pete's sake, he made a living in the City, convincing punters to part with their money. Yet the angry hunk of lard sitting next to him, and the blur of the verge passing by, knocked his concentration right off. *"Why does he need to know any of this shit? Can't we just have a civilized conversation?"* Tarquin felt exasperated. *"Oh well, here we go."* Taking a deep breath, he swept the hair off his face and replied as best he could.

"I want," he paused, "well I," a hint of hesitation, "I want," he cleared his throat, "to run a huge multi-national."

As soon as the words came out Tarquin winced.

"Shit. That's not ambitious enough to keep him happy."

"T… ten?" Tarquin stuttered. "I want to be the majority shareholder in ten multi-nationals. Make billions, dominate the competition. You know?"

"Damn it." That lacked ambition too. He could feel the Fat Man's ire building. "You know what?" Tarquin declared. "I want to be one of those billionaires whose got more power than the politicians. I want to own the politicians. You know? So they can't take a piss without asking me first. I want to have so much money it makes ordinary people feel sick, and I don't want to pay any tax." Tarquin had done everything in his power to recover, but it was not enough, and he knew it. His answers sounded pathetic even to his ears. So, he held his breath waiting for the explosion to come.

"Half-wit." The Fat Man tossed at him, pushing the Aston harder as his teeth and the gearbox crunched in harmony. If there had been an answer that could satisfy the distorted workings of the Fat Man's mind, this young man would be the last person to come up with it. And if by some miracle he did, it would be greeted with outright derision, simply because it came from him. The Fat Man was not in the habit of giving people a break. His job was to push the boy until he snapped, and then humiliate him. Tarquin's job was to keep his cool and not enrage the Fat Man so much that he crashed the car and killed them both. Tarquin was at his wits end with the Fat Man's bullying. Yes, his answer had been slightly unimaginative, but there was no need for all the negativity. The young man wanted to explode, to lash out at this despicable man, but he curbed his animal instincts and swallowed his pride. Patience was required. Tarquin had a plan, and it would not be long before he showed this bastard he was not as soft as he looked.

Tarquin awoke from his vengeful daydream as the Fat Man tore round a corner lined with rhododendron bushes.

"Oh God, what am I doing. Getting into this car was a bad idea." Thought Tarquin. The Aston shuddered, its smoking wheels failing to gain traction on the tarmac. The pinks and purples of the bushes became a blur, as the vehicle lurched sideways, kissing a stone wall to their right.

The Fat Man's expression did not change.
Tarquin's expression did not change.

Tarquin knew any signs of weakness, such as profuse sweating, bursting into tears or soiling himself, would encourage the driver to escalate his potentially fatal game. Even if the Fat Man possessed the driving skills he believed he did, at that speed he would not be able to control the car. Tarquin's fears materialised as the rear end of the Aston started to wobble and then slide into the right-hand lane. A red Massey Ferguson tractor was coming the other way, with a sprayer on the back. The Fat Man tried to coax the Aston to the left, but it would not respond. Now they were only twenty yards from the tractor, which had skidded to a halt, and the farmer was now struggling to get out of the cab. The impact and ensuing fireball was inevitable.

Then something extraordinary happened. Something most people never experience, and if they do it changes their life profoundly. Tarquin's world slowed down. The hairs on the back of his neck stood on end, as a soft, silent presence engulfed him and everything around him. His mind went silent, all thoughts disappearing from his head, and he began to watch the whole scene with him and the Fat Man unfold by itself. He was no longer Tarquin, he was space. He was no longer stressed out, he was free. His mind was no longer hammering away at him at it had done for as long as he could remember, it was silent. He was not a spiritual man, but he sensed a force he could not comprehend had arrived with the sole purpose of protecting him. He was moments from death and felt as calm and safe as he had ever done in his mother's arms.

He watched the Fat Man struggling with the steering wheel showing no emotion. As if he was visiting from another time, detatched from the drama.

Slam.

The Fat Man regained control of the car, missing the tractor by inches. It had all happened in a split second, but for Tarquin it had seemed to take an age. A slow and perfect sequence of events, inevitable in their success. Instead of taking the hint, this near miss seemed to fill the Fat Man with misplaced confidence, and he continued to push the Aston harder. Tarquin no longer cared, his experience of deep peace removing any hint of concern for his life or that of the driver. 'Hell drive' was far from over, but Tarquin did not mind. Following another vicious bend, the Fat Man straightened the car, but although he probably thought differently, he was no Michael Schumacher. He overcompensated at the next corner, and this time the rear end sent a couple of ramblers diving for cover.

"Bloody road hog," A pensioner shouted, as he picked himself out of a hedge, and the Fat Man laughed. A split second later they shot over a hump-backed bridge and the Aston's chassis became airborne. The vehicle flew over the blind summit like an Exocet guided missile, without the guidance. The low racing suspension was not designed to cope with such a heavy landing, and it knocked the wind out of Tarquin.

"Ooofff," he grunted, his face grimacing in pain. In an instant he returned to a normal reality.

The Fat Man did not seem to notice, or if he did, he certainly did not care.

"Please get me out of here," Tarquin prayed as he clutched his stomach and looked to the skies, but he had a feeling there more to endure. The Fat Man seemed to be in his own world, his angry eyes staring straight ahead, and his mind no doubt churning on some evil thought.

Most of the local wildlife was savvy enough to dive into the hedgerows before the Aston came into sight, but one young rabbit was too wet behind the ears to know any better. Oblivious to the threat speeding towards it, the rabbit sat alone in the middle of the road waiting to see what all the noise was about. The Fat Man spotted the bunny and began to chew his lower lip as he lined up the bonnet with the unfortunate beast. Tarquin prayed it would hop into the safety of the verge, but the bunny did not move. Instead, it sat looking at the car, transfixed.

The Fat Man hit the gas.

Thlumph.

"No more Bugs," the Fat Man laughed sadistically. Tarquin's heart sank and he closed his eyes. He felt disgusted by this man who could only feel joy when causing others pain.

CHAPTER 5

Puppy Love

Ernie's wildest dreams had come true, and the romance that followed was proof that opposites do, from time to time, attract. The shy, spotty redhead struck a chord in the heart of the athletic, seventeen-year-old warrior babe, and it did not take long before both of them had fallen for each other. Summer was in the air, and they began their very own version of Bonnie and Clyde, with Karen opening up a whole new world to Ernie. She was his unicorn, showing him a mysterious world he would never have visited by himself. Karen taught Ernie how to fight, and most importantly how to win. Even with crutches he learned to look after himself, and a quiet inner confidence grew. As the first girl who had ever wanted to spend any time with Ernie, it was easy for Karen to lead him astray, and she took great pleasure in doing so. Every day they met up after school and hung out together. Ernie had never been in trouble before, and was quite happy to follow Karen's lead, with neither of them giving any thought to the consequences.

It turned out that despite their very different personalities, Ernie and Karen had a lot in common. They were both orphans who had lost their mothers in their teenaged years, and neither of them knew their father. They were both loners who believed life was against them, and neither felt like they fitted in. She faced her challenges with overconfidence and aggression, and he faced his by keeping his head down and trying to avoid trouble. Their challenges pulled them close, and they instinctively trusted each other, spending more and more time in each other's company.

Karen taught Ernie how to break into anything cheap with four wheels, and he was a most willing student. After a few nervous attempts, he became a pretty good car thief who could jump start most vehicles if he had enough time. Karen also passed on her shoplifting skills, which was handy when they needed supplies for their excursions. Ernie learnt how to distract shopkeepers whilst Karen nipped around the back and pilfered alcohol and cigarettes. Karen led, and

Ernie followed, and that was the way they liked it.

o o o

"Wake up boy, where the hell are you anyway?" the Fat Man goaded. Tarquin swallowed hard but did not look at the driver.

"This is a total nightmare! I've got to get out of here," he thought desperately.

"My God, if running over a rabbit upsets you this much, how do you expect to get anywhere in life? Life is pain, and it's good to inflict a little now and again, it keeps you sharp. Besides, there are too many rabbits in this part of the world. Just like people. Too many rabbits in Surrey, too many people on the planet. Whose gonna miss one?"

"Oh my God," thought Tarquin, but held his tongue.

"Am I that bad? I don't think so. You eat meat, you just don't have the nerve to kill it for yourself," continued the Fat Man.

"You didn't take that rabbit home and cook it for supper, sir," Tarquin blurted out, immediately regretting his insolence.

"I know. I'm not hungry." The Fat Man smiled, enjoying the challenge. "Look boy, I don't like rabbits and I don't like people, but I do have some redeeming features."

"Really?" Tarquin thought, *"I hadn't noticed."*

"I'm not that bad. A little overzealous at times, but we all have our faults," the Fat Man gloated.

"You extort people for a living. You hurt them, you steal from them, and goodness knows what other crimes you've committed. You are a bad man." Tarquin wanted to say but did not.

"For instance. I'm no racist. Surely that's something?" The Fat Man asked but did not wait for a reply. "Racism is the tool of weak, little men who've had sand kicked in their faces. Do you really think I have anything in common with morons who tattoo Union Jacks all over their bodies, and beat the hell out of some poor bastard from another country?" Sweat oozed from the Fat Man's pores, and globules of spit flew out his mouth as he ranted. "Lonely little men. I despise them. I remember they used to hang around pubs at closing time. They'd down ten pints of lager and attack anyone who wasn't born within ten miles of them. True warriors, as long as they outnumber their victims by five to one," he spat sarcastically. "I used to love fighting them. I never lost you know? Not once. No boy, I am no racist. Racism is the product of fear, and fear is something I have not felt for many years."

"Is it possible he never feels afraid?" Tarquin wondered. It seemed unlikely. Everyone had their

Achilles heel, no matter how brave, stupid or shut down they were. He had seen enough of life to know the things people deny most furiously, are most often the things they fear the most. Pausing to draw breath, the Fat Man turned to look at his passenger.

"No, I am no racist. I hate white people too."

"Perhaps now he'll slow down?" Tarquin hoped.

Wishful thinking.

"Getting back to my original question, and I don't want to have to repeat myself again. How rich do you want to be by the time you're thirty-five?"

"Oh no. Not again," Tarquin had hoped the Fat Man's rantings might have distracted him from his earlier line of interrogation.

"I was asked the same question by my father when I was your age. Do you know what I told him?" He boomed. "I told him I would be so filthy rich the food at my dinner parties would be served on the naked bodies of famous supermodels. I would be so obscenely wealthy my guests would snort lines of cocaine from their breasts between courses. Of course, once the party was over, I also made the models clean the toilets and scrub the floors. There are few things more satisfying than watching the world's most successful beauties cleaning a toilet. Vain people really hate to clean toilets," he chortled. "I told him my guests would be the most influential members of society, and I would covertly video them all. My father was not an easy man to please, but he liked my answer a great deal. Soon after I had told him of my ingenious plan, I held hoolies more debauched than you could ever dream of. I must say," his tone softened as he recalled fond memories of his younger years, "it took a great deal of Champagne to persuade some of my guests to play along, but they did, and the footage has proved useful ever since. I am never too far from the ear of certain Members of Parliament who sold me their soul in the seventies."

Screech.

Another near miss, but the Fat Man was not ruffled. He was not going to die today. Not today. No chance.
"When I ask you a question, I expect you to give me a bloody good answer. Not on the third attempt, or the second, but immediately." His voice hardened. "You have to aim high. My God, you've only got one life, so you have to go for what you really want. If you want something, make it big, and if you don't get it, go out and take it anyway. It takes balls to be a big shot. Bloody hell, boy, where are your balls?"

The younger man did not react. He was used to the abuse. The Aston skidded to a halt behind a queue of cars. Its treads smoking as the Fat Man stopped inches from the bumper of a brand-new Cortina, cursing as he was forced to crawl his way around a perfectly good bend. An array of box like cars that frequented middle England in the eighties queued ahead of them impatiently.

"Who allowed these morons on the road? Look at them, they're a bloody disgrace," the Fat Man raged, turning his head to look at his passenger. "You have got to distinguish yourself from these idiots. Don't let the nothingness of this country drag you down. Lord help us all. Look at these parasites. They're the forgotten generation. Working their fingers to the bone, so they can keep up with the Jones's next door. They've sold their souls so they can own a shitty little house in the country, a shitty new car, and take a shitty holiday in the Algarve twice a year. Look at them!" The Fat Man's face contorted with disgust, as though he was staring at a particularly grizzly road accident. "Not one bit of imagination between the lot of them. The walking dead. Oblivious to their pathetic existence, they believe their tragic state of normality is success." His brow furrowed and his voice dropped. "Heed my words, mediocrity truly is the greatest threat to our civilization."

Tarquin looked at him but said nothing.

"Do you know the worst thing? They lie down and accept it.

'Yeah, my job's pretty dull, I haven't had sex with my wife for months, but if I keep going, I might get a raise next year. Then I can buy that new Mondeo, and maybe she'll give me a blow job on my birthday?'" the Fat Man mocked in a whiny voice. "Bloody zombies, they can't even remember their dreams, let alone follow them. Enough!"

He hit the gas and snaked his way around the line of cars, unruffled by the blind bends.

"You are not going to die today. Not today."

"Oh shit," mouthed Tarquin, uttering the shortest prayer in the world, well aware that hell drive was far from over.

Back on the open road Tarquin breathed a sigh of relief, and the Fat Man went on and on about whatever soulless topic he took a fancy to. Tarquin did not pay any attention to anything he said. There was only so much ranting he could endure in one day, and he had put up with it for as long as he could remember. After all, Tarquin was the Fat Man's only son.

o o o

It was a hot July evening and Karen and Ernie

were up to no good. The young couple stood next to a corner shop in a run-down district of Newcastle, smoking cigarettes and trying not to look suspicious. Karen was wearing a tight pair of hot pants and a red bikini top, looking sporty and tantalising. Ernie was wearing brown corduroys and a yellow Hawaiian shirt, looking like he had just escaped from the local day unit. A red Ford Escort was parked outside the shop, it's bonnet too hot for them to lean on. The air was still, and the pavement so soft that a pair of stilettos would have left their heel print in the tarmac. An old lady with a blue rinse and a Zimmer frame slowly made her way towards the shop. Other than her, no one was around. As they stood on the pavement, Karen kept one eye on the car, making sure the owner was nowhere to be seen.

Three quarters of an hour later, Ernie and Karen were driving to St. Mary's Island in the red Ford Escort, joking and laughing at yet another success.

"We'll give the car back later," Karen winked. "We're just borrowing it."

St. Mary's island was a popular destination for young lovers, and just a short joy ride from Fenham. Karen skidded the Escort to a halt in a car park next to the island.

"Come on slow coach," she giggled as she kicked open her car door, laughing as Ernie struggled to open his. He got out slowly and hobbled after her, as she disappeared into the night.

"I've got a place I want to show you Ernie. I think you're gonna like it, if it's not too scary for you," Karen teased, as she cartwheeled in the sand. Whipping her strong legs over her head without a care in the world.

"Here it is," Karen declared, as she found an opening in the rocks hidden behind thick gorse bushes. Creeping around the thorny shrubs, they crawled inside.

"Wow," gasped Ernie, as the small opening became a cavern large enough to stand up in. The walls were wet, glistening in the scarce light that the entrance allowed in.

"Isn't this cool? I love it here, it's so secret," said Karen, her voice echoing in the cave. They sat down, side by side in the darkness. It was so exciting to be in a cave with Karen. Just the two of them and nobody else around. Ernie could feel her warmth against his arm, and the small movements of her breath. Were they going to do it for the first time? He felt he should make a move, but something did not feel right, this place started to give him the creeps. Then Karen leaned over to kiss him and he started to panic.

"What are you ganna do now schools over?" Ernie asked frantically. "Are you going to try and get a job?"

"Erm. I think I'm going to become a mechanic." Karen replied, a look consternation on her face. "I don't think I'm cut out for a girly job, but I'd like to know my way around car engines. D'you think I'd look good in overalls?" she said, the glint still in her eye.

"Of course you would. You look good in anything, even a chef's outfit," Ernie replied, looking over his shoulder nervously. As time went on the cave became darker and more foreboding. The drip, drip, drip of water from the roof unnerved him. "Kazza, ah don't wanna sound like a wimp, like, but it's kind of creepy in here," he shivered.

"Oh, Ernie you are such a big baby," Karen sighed, not bothering to hide her disappointment. "Okay, let's get back to the car."

"Shit, ah screwed that one up," thought Ernie, as he trudged back to the car park a long way behind Karen.

As they lay on the bonnet of the Escort, staring into the clear night sky, Ernie's worries vanished. It was as if he and Karen were the only people in the world.

"Ah can't believe how many stars there are," gasped Ernie. "There's millions of them. More than ah can count."

"I know," Karen was quiet for a while, staring into the dark space above them. "It's weird, but when I look at them it feels like they're inside me. It's like I go on forever and stretch out past the stars. It feels really nice. Like none of my worries are worth bothering about, you know what I mean?"

"Yeh, kind of," said Ernie, not wanting her to stop.

"Do you know some of those stars don't even exist anymore? They burnt out millions of years ago. You can see them shine, but the star is gone. Isn't that cool?"

"Wow," Ernie's heart pounded, *"not only beautiful, but clever too."*

"We learnt it in physics, it's about the only thing I remember," Karen laughed.

"Do you think there are people living up there? People like us?"

"Yes, I do," she replied. "There must be, there are so many stars. Why would we be the only ones?"

Ernie focused on a bright, blinking star, imagining how it would be with cities, bridges, dogs and perhaps squirrels on it?

"I'm sure we're not the only ones. There must be beings out there. Beings who can do stuff, build things, think for themselves," Karen turned to face Ernie, and looked at him with an intensity in her blue eyes. "Beings who can fall in love."

Ernie gulped, nervous and excited at the same

time. What did she mean, 'fall in love'? More importantly, did he have a condom with him? He felt so out of his depth and searched his brain for something to say.

"There are angels up there too. Me mam told me when ah was little," he blurted out. "She told me to look up at the stars if ah ever felt lonely, and to know ah was being looked after. She said the angels were watching over me, like, and that they would take care of me."

"Maybe our mums are angels now? Maybe they're watching over us? I hope that's true Ernie, I really do."

"Me too. What, with all me bad luck and all," Ernie frowned.

"Ernie," Karen snapped, "you've gotta stop putting yourself down and start believing in yourself. You're the sweetest guy I've ever met, and you're brave. You took a kicking to save a family of flies, and there's not a lot of people who would do that."

"Okay, Kazza, ah'll try," he nodded obediently. "Me Mam once told me that life is like a poker game. We can't choose the cards we're dealt, but we can choose how we play them. You've shown me that Kazza. Your cards were pretty shitty but look at you. You make the most out of everything. You're showing me how to play, but ah'm not doing such a great job."

"I don't think your hand is as shitty as you think. You just don't see what you've got."

"Ah've got you," said Ernie, reaching into one of his pockets. "Anyways, enough about me. Ah've got something ah want to give you. Close your eyes and give us your hand," and she did. Ernie fastened a small, red watch to her arm, fumbling with the strap. He took a moment to admire how it looked on her lovely wrist and was happy. "You can open your eyes now," he finally said.

Karen made a sound of delight.

"It's a Mini Mouse watch. Look, ah've got a Mickey Mouse one," he said as he waved his wrist in Karen's face. Ah got it for me tenth birthday, like. Now, we're a pair."

"That's so cool Ernie," Karen replied, beaming. I'm never going to take it off.

"Well, it's not waterproof, dummy. So if you wanna take a shower in the next year it's a good idea to take it off," Ernie smiled.

"Always the joker, eh?" Karen punched him on the arm and then rolled off the bonnet of the borrowed car. She opened one of the back doors and hopped inside. "Come on," she giggled, as Ernie struggled to get down onto the sand. "Leave your crutches cripple, you won't need them." She teased him as usual, but there was something different in her voice, something passionate and excited. As he closed the car door, Karen lent forward and kissed him on the lips. The kiss was as soft as the caress of a flower, and then another followed, and another, and another. Each kiss sent Ernie deeper into a haze of teenaged lust. Finally he was going to get laid!

Ernie was a virgin and had never even kissed a girl before he met Karen. His only reference to the mysterious act of sex were porn videos he had seen at school. The cool boys had watched them in their common room, and Ernie had sneaked a look at them through the window. For a little while he tried to copy the well-hung, German porn stars. He lavished sloppy kisses all over Karen's face, as if he was in the process of eating her. He gripped her bum as tightly as he could, grunting for no reason as he pinched her skin.

"Ow, relax Ernie," Karen squealed. "What are you doing? Jeez, let me handle this."

"Thank God," thought Ernie. *"This is not my area of expertise."*

Karen looked Ernie in the eyes with a depth and tenderness he had never felt. She took hold of her bikini top and smoothly lifted it over her head. Her perfect breasts bounced a little and came to rest only inches from his face. Ernie froze. Karen took one of his hands and placed it on her bosom, and then lent forward and kissed him on the lips.

"Gently," she whispered, and Ernie dropped his porn star impersonation and settled for a lot of hugging and prodding. There in the back of an old Ford Escort, with the Milky Way looking down on the young lovers, and the sound of the waves lapping at the shoreline, Karen and Ernie made love for the first time.

The occasion quickly got the better of him and having fumbled around on the back seat for a couple of minutes, Ernie yelped with delight and collapsed in Karen's arms. His face a picture of deep contentment and joy. For Ernie it had been the most mind-blowing experience he had ever had. For Karen it was sweet and intimate but did not last quite as long as she had hoped. However, practice makes perfect, and in the next few weeks they did a lot of practicing.

o o o

The Fat Man had at one time or another broken almost every law there is to break. His crimes ranged from bigamy, to arson, to grand theft, to murder. He was as far away from goodness as a human being could be, lacking any semblance of basic decency. His only redeeming feature, if one looked very hard indeed, was that he was not a coward. The Fat Man grabbed life in a vice like grip and squeezed every last drop out of it. His exaggerated proportions were the most obvious by-product of following this hedonistic philosophy to the letter. He was a man who did everything in excess, and somehow got away with it. His father had been the British Minister for Justice throughout South Africa's darkest years of Apartheid. He was brutal man who had taken great pleasure in beating his son whenever he was angry or bored, which was all too often.

"Look at these sad little creatures, they'd be better off dead," the Fat Man declared as he played chicken with the oncoming traffic. Tarquin noticed his father cast his eyes towards the Aston's glovebox. It was in the glovebox that the most accessible weapon in the Fat Man's arsenal was stored. It was an Uzi 9mm machine gun which was his pride and joy. Tarquin was unsure of what the Fat man was thinking, but he hoped frustration did not get the better of his father. Tarquin thought he was quite capable of opening fire on the other drivers if they annoyed him enough, and he did not want to get caught in the middle of that. The Fat Man claimed he only had the Uzi for protection. Protection from whom Tarquin was not sure, for it would take an army to take this man down. The young stockbroker tried to reassure himself that no matter how angry his father got he would not open fire on the other drivers, believing it crueler to let them live.

"Let them eek out their half-dead existence, crawling back to their semi-detached holes in the ground," he spat bitterly, and he meant every word he said. "Tarquin are you listening to me?" the Fat Man yelled from behind the steering wheel.

"Yes Sir!" Tarquin replied, trying not to flinch.

"Do you think I called you Tarquin because I liked the name? Do you? Well, I didn't. It's a ridiculous name. It's weak. The first time I laid eyes on you I saw weakness. So I called you Tarquin, in the hope you would be bullied for it and it might toughen you up. This may seem a little harsh, but I was doing it for your own good. There is no place for weakness in this world. None whatsoever."

Tarquin did not know what to say.

"I didn't have time to deal with you myself when you were growing up, too much business, too much travelling, too many other things I wanted to do. Life is short Tarquin, I had to get my priorities right. I must say I'm glad your mother took on that responsibility. You were a pathetic child, and she was a pathetic woman. A perfect match."

Bam. Bam.

Out of nowhere, both barrels, full scale attack. Tarquin had never liked his name, and true to the Fat Man's wishes he *had* been picked on at school because of it. But to think his twisted father had called him

Tarquin for the sole reason that it would make his life a misery?

"Insane," thought Tarquin, feeling a dark and familiar hatred welling up inside him. What he really took objection to the Fat Man insulting his late mother. The old man could say what he wanted about Tarquin, but not her, he owed her everything. She had been the only one who had protected him and shown him love. Throughout his early childhood his father had slowly but surely destroyed her. Pulling her apart piece by piece, year after year, with his womanizing, and his lies, and his unkind words.

Tarquin's parents had met not long after his father had suffered a broken heart. His mother had fallen pregnant and they had married soon after that. It became clear that Nigel was still in love with his ex, and there was no room for her. In fact, she was only in the way. It had not taken long for his infidelity and wicked words to break her heart, and a few years later they had broken her spirit. Tarquin was all that remained of their few unhappy years together. He loathed his father more than anyone else on earth, for as long as he could remember, this ogre had only caused him pain. He recalled the tearful pleas of his mother when his father was letting his blows reign down on either her or Tarquin. The Fat Man had no interest in spending time with his son, preferring to chase women and build his evil empire. For the past few years their only contact had been in the cockpit of the Aston.

Tarquin shook off these painful memories, right now there was no time for dwelling on the past. If he kept his cool and got through this drive in one piece, he would have his sweet revenge on the rabid animal who had destroyed his childhood. Sliding his hand to the discrete leather holster hugging his chest, Tarquin unbuttoned it quietly. Feeling the cold metal against the palm of his hand, a drop of sweat trickled down his temple. He was so tempted to end his father's sickening life. *"If only I had the guts, I'd kill the fat bastard right now,"* he schemed. However, that was not the plan, and Tarquin was not going to ruin weeks of careful preparation by losing his cool. His pistol was a last resort in case things went south, and he had nothing to gain by making it into a murder weapon. Reluctantly, Tarquin slid it back into its holster, buttoned it up and moved his hand back onto his lap.

"I know what you're thinking. You want to kill me because I spoke ill of your mother. You are *so* predictable," the Fat Man mocked, shaking his head disparagingly.

"How does he do that? How does he know what I'm thinking? Am I really that easy to read?"

The endless drive went on and his father's face got redder and redder as it did. Sweat oozed from every orifice, and the hatred that spewed from his mouth intensified with every mile that passed. Tarquin was disgusted by the sight of this bloated man, who looked like an uglier version of Jabba the Hut on speed.

"Tarquin," the Fat Man barked, "there is something else I want to tell you."

It was unlikely to be a speech on the need to protect the indigenous tribes of Brazil, thought Tarquin laconically.

"I screwed Victoria Delacroix last night," the Fat Man boasted.

"Victoria Delacroix, the supermodel?"

"Then I kicked her out of my hotel room and told her never to come back. She blubbed like a baby, heartbroken that I didn't want anything to do with her. So beautiful yet so disappointing. I think I prefer plainer girls, they try harder," he mused, overtaking on a tight corner then skidding the car back to his side of the road, just in time to avoid a collision with a truck. This game of cat and mouse continued, with the Fat Man dodging the oncoming vehicles that presented themselves on a Sunday afternoon on the A3 between Haslemere and Putney.

He continued to boast of female conquests, bribery, extortion and murder, as his passenger smiled with his mouth but not his eyes. Satisfied that the Fat Man was absorbed in his ranting, Tarquin slowly moved his hand into his other jacket pocket.

"Good," his Dictaphone was still recording. The old bastard was on a roll. Tarquin would let him think he was in charge. Then, when the Fat Man least expected it, he would pounce and do what he should have done years ago. *"This is exactly what I want,"* Tarquin thought. *"Keep talking, Fat Man. Keep talking."*

o o o

A chaotically smitten summer followed, with the besotted couple making love whenever and wherever they could. Borrowed cars, cinemas and a bright-red telephone box saw the fervour of their *l'amour*. Ernie continued to shower his Juliet with gifts, taking bigger risks to get them, and Karen gave more of her heart to her lover as every day passed. As a team they were stronger than the two individuals they had been, and Ernie felt a surge of self-confidence he never knew he had. He began to stick up for himself and got into a couple of fights, which thanks to Karen he won by the skin of his teeth. Word got around and the bullies soon stopped picking on him.

The only other significant male in Karen's life had been her stepfather, and he had left her shortly after her mother had died, without bothering to say goodbye. He was an angry man with a short temper and quick fists, who had beaten both Karen and her mother. Ernie was quite the opposite. He would never lay a finger on her. He may not have had John Travolta's torso, but he was the kindest guy she had ever met, and most importantly, he made her laugh. How he made her laugh. Of course, Ernie was not perfect. Karen hated it when he blew his nose with a dirty old handkerchief at mealtimes. However, she could forgive him these *faux pas*, because he was attentive and caring and wanted the best for her. Every week he gave her flowers he had stolen from the local graveyard, proving beyond any doubt that romance was not dead.

Despite his new found happiness, Ernie was far from over his mother's death. Sometimes waves of guilt and sadness would crash into him and pull him into the depths. Having Karen in his life made his grief so much easier to bear. She had a tough exterior but was softer than she let on, and she knew all too well the pain of losing a mother. Karen was the shoulder Ernie could cry on when his pain became too much to carry alone, and sometimes the tears would run down her cheeks as well.

As the weeks passed, Ernie thought less about Babs and began to look forward to the rest of his life, which he secretly hoped would be with Karen. She had more passion than anyone he had ever met, and he loved that. Her passion meant life was not always straightforward, but the drama and excitement of going out with a fireball more than made up for it. For the most part he and Karen got on like a house on fire, but every so often they impersonated one.

"You think I'm fat?" Karen shouted, unable to hold back the volcano which was erupting.

"Ah, no pet, that's not what ah said, like," Ernie backtracked.

"So, Mr. Skinny, what exactly *did* you say?" seethed Karen as she stood in front of her bedroom mirror.

"Well, just that your bum."

"What about it?"

"It sticks out in that dress. That's all."

A perfume bottle flew past Ernie's head.

"You arrogant prick! You think my hips are fat don't you?"

A lipstick smacked him in the forehead.

"Ow." Not fat, no. They just look a bit bigger," he cringed.

Wrong answer.

Karen's hairbrush cracked him in the ribs.

"Cheeky bastard. You've never liked my hips, have you?"

"Oh, jeez Kazza, ah love your hips. Can't we just forget about this?"

"Yeah, okay, I'll forget about the fact that you don't fancy me anymore."

"But, pet, ah do…"

Ernie's social hand grenades and Karen's feistiness fired up the passion, and when he was not dodging flying cosmetics, Ernie felt invincible. With Karen by his side he knew that nothing could stop him. However, unbeknownst to the young lovers it was not only their euphoric summer that was drawing to a close. Autumn was fast approaching, and an ill wind was blowing in from the bitter North Sea. The weather would change and so would their fortunes. Ernie and Karen's Paradise was about to be well and truly lost.

CHAPTER 6

Paradise Lost

As the Fat Man floored the accelerator once more, leaving the car stinking of molten rubber, his thoughts drifted back two decades to another time, another fast car, and a head on collision with a tree.

"Damn you John Malone, you bastard," he thought, his face twisting into a painful scowl, but he refused to dwell on the memory for long, it hurt too much. So, he kept driving faster, harder, and angrier.

"Which girl are you seeing, boy?" the Fat Man roared over the engine.

"Zoe Einhart. The same girl I've been seeing for the last three years. You know, my fiancé?" Tarquin roared back. "Or perhaps you've been too busy to absorb that minor detail?" he added under his breath, his knuckles white from gripping the door handle.

"Oh Lord, not that silly cow. I thought I told you to get rid of her months ago?"

"You did," Tarquin muttered.

"For God's sake," the Fat Man shook his head. "When are you going to learn?"

"Learn what?"

"Do you know how stupid you are marrying Zoe?"

Tarquin was not aware of how stupid he was, but he suspected he was about to find out.

"Obviously, I'm not one to lecture."

"Of course not," thought Tarquin, but held his tongue.

"Do you know nothing of the importance of choosing your mate wisely? Your fiancé is a poor choice. She's not bright at all. If I'm honest, she's slow. Not so many sandwiches in her lunchbox, if you know what I mean? intelligence is vital if you want win in life and she hasn't got it. Yes, I know she's pretty, and has some qualities that people value far too highly."

"Like kindness, love, and patience?"

"Yes, yes," The Fat Man agreed, rolling his eyes, "but those are irrelevant in the war of life. She's not bright enough for you. She doesn't understand the importance of winning, and she makes you softer instead of carving you into a real man."

"You don't understand," Tarquin countered. "The world isn't like that anymore. Just because *you* have a battle inside your head does not mean that everyone else is at war."

"Yes, yes. More of your hippy bullshit. Whether you like it or not she doesn't have the qualities necessary to be your mate."

"Like cruelty, ambition and bitterness?" Tarquin scowled, trusting the noise of the engine would stop his father from hearing.

"I suggest you rid yourself of your bride to be," the Fat Man bellowed, losing patience with his stubborn son. This was too much for Tarquin to take.

"I'm a grown up," he shouted back. "You can't control my life. Not anymore."

"Oh yes? Well, I can certainly influence it a great deal."

Tarquin ignored his father's poorly veiled threat.

"I'm not going to give him the satisfaction," he thought. This pleased the Fat Man. Perhaps the boy was learning?

"As you know Tarquin, I don't work for the Red Cross. In my line of business, if someone decides to be difficult, I bury them."

Tarquin's ears pricked up. Was the old man about to give him something juicy?

"How many people have you taken out in your time?" Tarquin asked, hoping to spur him on.

"Ah," the Fat Man purred, eager to impress his son with sinister stories of his twisted life, "well, I think it's a smidgen shy of eighteen. I was twenty when I did my first. I remember it well. He was a huge man. Over six foot four, a nightclub bouncer, and I beat him to death with a steel pipe. He deserved it. He was coming on to a girlfriend of mine, great legs she had, great legs.

There have been politicians, of course. The unique thing about killing politicians is that the deaths have to look like accidents. God knows I don't want an entire police force coming after me, just because an overzealous politician got in my way. You can't be too careful, you know?" he boasted. The Fat Man's appearance transformed remarkably as he reminisced. The anger that had consumed him for most of the drive was replaced with a loathsome delight in his own despicable crimes. His voice hushed to a steady purr as he recounted details of the evil deeds he had orchestrated over the years. This was exactly what Tarquin wanted. His father's vanity getting the better of him.

Names, dates, motives and methods. As the Fat Man continued, he gave Tarquin more ammunition than he could have hoped for. His driving slowed, and if he appeared to be winding up a story, Tarquin would ask another question, keeping his father talking for as long as he could. He had finally succeeded in exploiting his father's inflated sense of self-importance, but timing was everything. He knew he could only keep the old man talking for so long, before he caught on to what his son was up to.

"You've got balls," Tarquin complemented, trying to sound genuine.

Suddenly, the Fat Man hit the accelerator again, his thick fingers squeezing the steering wheel as he stared menacingly at his son. Despite the oncoming traffic bearing down on them he insisted on looking straight at Tarquin. An icicle of fear entered the young man's chest and his throat tightened. Had he gone too far?

"I know *I've* got balls," the Fat Man snapped. "What I want to know is, where are *your* balls you little bastard? Do you think you can trick me into spewing my guts, while you record the whole conversation on the Dictaphone hidden in your jacket, and then blackmail me? You're as subtle as a flying sledgehammer. It's the oldest trick in the book. I would have expected a little more from you. Not a great deal more, but a bit."

"*Oh shit. I've* been rumbled," Thought Tarquin, scrambling to regain his composure. He had known this might happen, but that did not stop him feeling like a cornered rat. Now he only had one option and it was not a desirable one. He had to go on the offensive.

"My balls are exactly where Mother Nature intended them to be," he erupted in his most fearsome voice, which was not fearsome at all. "The question is, where are yours, Fat Man?"

No reply came.

"Actually, I can answer that. They're right here," he declared holding out his clenched fist. As Tarquin swallowed a volcano of panic, he did what he had prayed he would never have to do. In one swift movement, he unbuttoned his holster, removed the revolver, and held the cold metal to his father's head. "Perhaps *this* will convince you I'm serious. Now pull the fuck over."

Not one to obey orders, the Fat Man dropped the car into third and the rear end locked. It spun sideways into the middle of the road, missing a Harley Davidson by inches. Tarquin continued to hold the pistol to his father's temple, relieved that the car's vibrations concealed the trembling of his hand. "This conversation puts your balls right in the palm of *my* hand," He shouted hollowly. The Fat Man turned his head, looking at Tarquin as if he was worth less than a cockroach in the kitchen of a tenement flat. It was a look that would wither the most seasoned of adversaries and drove an icicle of fear into his son's heart. Tarquin wanted to beg for mercy, but it was too late for that.

"Oh, I know you're serious," the Fat Man replied in a patronising tone, "but right now that is beside the point." He was actually quite impressed by Tarquin's exploits but would never dream of showing it. Perhaps the cockroach was not as pathetic as he looked? Perhaps he might one day be a chip off the old block? "You think you're in control of this situation, don't you? But do you see me trembling? Do I look faint? Gosh Tarquin, stop being such a fool." How anyone could sound bored whilst driving at 120 miles per hour with a gun to their head Tarquin had no idea, but his father sounded bored. "But let me humour you a little. Grant me one last wish before you bravely fill me with lead. I have a question."

"What question?" Tarquin did not like the way this was going.

"Have you heard of a man called Reggie Kray?"

"I'm not bluffing you know. I *will* shoot you."

"I won't ask you again boy," the Fat Man commanded, "have you heard of Reggie Kray?"

"Yes, some gangster from the Sixties. Now shut up," Tarquin could feel the advantage slipping away from him. "If you don't pull over, I *am* going to kill you. Do you understand?"

"Yes, yes, yes," the Fat Man scoffed, "but before

you do, I must tell you a story." The Fat Man's purr returned as he settled into another monologue. "Reggie Kray was renowned for his 'cigarette' punch. Cigarette punch? you ask. What does that have to do with anything? Well, bear with me a minute. A bit like me, Reggie liked to be in control, and he didn't like to be pushed around."

Tarquin felt utterly powerless. The gun in his hand might as well have been a bunch of carnations, but he continued to hold it against the Fat Man's temple.

"From time to time, he needed to set an example for people who had crossed the line. A violent one. He had a favourite way of doing this, Tarquin. Do you know what that was?"

Silence.

"He'd offer his victim a cigarette, which for obvious reasons would always be accepted. Then he'd hold out a lighter, which would also be accepted. As his victim lent forward, relaxing his jaw to suck on the flame, Mr. Kray would throw a vicious left hook at his chin. This would break it into pieces and knock him out cold. You see, when the jaw's relaxed, even the softest blow will shock the inner ear and bingo, you've got one very unconscious person."

"Why don't you shut up," Tarquin shrieked, his nerve well and truly gone. "For once in your life, shut up! I've got a gun and you are telling me bedtime fucking stories? For God's sake, pull over!"

The Fat Man kept driving.

"Yes, you do have a gun, but that's not *my* problem."

"It's a big fucking problem if I use it."

"We both know you're not going to do that. You can't blackmail a dead man, can you?"

"No, but I can kill a man I hate."

"I'm not so sure, Tarquin. Perhaps you could? But then you'd have to deal with being a murderer. You'd have to live with the fact that you'd killed your own father in cold blood. That you'd become just like him."

"Why won't you pull over? What is your problem?" Tarquin screamed again.

"Do you really want to know?"

"Yes, I bloody do!"

"Well, its' the fact that you don't smoke." Then the crocodile smiled and threw a left jab at his son, catching him squarely on the jaw, knocking him out...

Cold.

o o o

Ernie sat on his mother's old sofa enjoying a quiet evening in front of the television. The sofa was covered in embroidered daffodils she had lovingly created when she was still alive, and it was Ernie's favourite place in the world to sit.

"She would have loved Karen, like," he thought, as a tear welled up and rolled down his cheek. It had been an intense three months and although he had enjoyed every minute he had spent with Karen, it was good to have some time on his own. Sometimes he felt guilty for falling in love when he should have been mourning his mother's death. But in the same way that his mother had sheltered him from an unloving world, Karen had protected him from the worst of the pain of her passing. He was no academic, but he was bright enough to know that being with Karen *had* saved him, at least for now. Ernie blew his nose fiercely and then wiped his eyes with his grubby handkerchief, smiling at the thought of how much it would have annoyed Karen. Limping over to one of the kitchen cupboards he grabbed the last packet of *Monster Munch* crisps and curled back up on the sofa. Comfort food and an episode of *Kung Fu* was enough to take his mind off missing Babs.

That week's episode affected Ernie more deeply than normal. Watching the mysterious monk travel from city to city, righting wrongs and punishing bullies for their crimes, struck a chord with Ernie. There was something about doing good in the world, when it was easier to do bad, that made him think about his own life. Was it fair stealing from families struggling to make a living selling sweets and cigarettes in battered corner shops? Was stealing cars really such a good idea? Was he making the world a better place or was he adding to the suffering of hard-working people?

His thoughts were interrupted by the peaceful monk punching an evil cowboy through a door with little effort. Then the monk began to lecture the man on the error of his ways. The dazed cowboy, his resolve weakened by the effortless grace and hard-hitting words of the Kung Fu master, got the message and repented. Ernie wanted to be that fearless monk, but these days he feared he was closer to becoming the despicable cowboy, and things never went well for such cowboys. Ernie was walking in the wrong direction, and his question should not have been, was it right or wrong? It should have been, did he have the courage to turn around and walk another way?

The doorbell rang, as jarring as usual, and Ernie stood up as if he had been hit by lightning. His weakest leg, which had gone numb with pins and needles, buckled under his weight and he fell crashing to the floor.

"Damn it!" he cursed and using the sofa to get

to his feet he hopped over to the front door. Karen was standing on the doorstep looking radiant, a broad smile plastered across her pretty face.

"Hello Ernie," she beamed.

"Hello love," he replied vacantly as he rubbed his backside.

"I've got something to tell you. Are you gonna let me in?" she said a little hesitantly.

"Ah've got a sore arse, babe," Ernie replied, not noticing this was a very important moment for Karen. One of those moments when it was vital for boyfriends to pay close attention to their girlfriends. Karen squeezed past him and pulled the door shut, her smile fading fast. "Ah divn't understand how yoose don't care this, like. Me leg might be seriously injured. Ah can't feel anything below me bum," Ernie whined, turning to face her. "Shit!" he shouted as he lost his balance once again and crashing into a bannister, and then a wall, and ended up in a pathetic heap on the floor. Karen's gaze rested to the mess sitting on the shaggy hall carpet and she frowned.

"Ern, come on, get up. There's nothing wrong with your bum. Your legs gone to sleep that's all. That's what happens when you sit in front of the telly all night," she said as she cleared her throat. Stretching out a hand she pulled Ernie to his feet and lead him back to the living room. She looked at him hard and took a moment to compose herself. "I've got something important to tell you, some good news," her face was flushed with embarrassment. "Well, I hope it's good news? Right now, when I think about it, it's all a bit scary." Karen's gaze intensified. "Ernie, you *do* like me, don't you? I mean, *really* like me?"

"Of course, pet. Ah've never, lo…, erm, liked anyone the way ah like you," he replied, testing his weight on his weaker leg. He wanted to say 'love' but did not dare.

Karen took a deep breath.

"Ernie, I'm, well, I mean, we're going to have a baby."

Ernie's brain stopped, and the world started to unfold in slow motion. His mind went blank and he was lost for words. Staring straight back at his true love, he tried to compute what she had just said.

"Ernie, Ernie!" Karen continued, her voice high pitched and anxious. "Did you hear what I said? I'm pregnant, you're going to be a dad."

Ernie so wanted to say the right thing, but it took time for news like this to sink in. It took longer for it to be processed, and even longer for a suitable response to be given to the love of his life. Rather than taking her in her arms, giving her a hug and telling her he was over the moon, he continued to stare at Karen, the blank expression not moving from his face. "Ernie,"

Karen's eyes welled up, "can't you do more than stand there gawping at me with your mouth hanging open? Say something, for God's sake, anything."

What seemed like minutes but was only seconds passed, and finally Ernie stammered,

"B... but Kazza, you can't be pregnant."

The look of disappointment on Karen's face would have caused a dozen red roses to wilt.

"Wrong answer," Ernie thought and began to panic. He knew what he wanted to say, or that he wanted to say the right thing, but his mouth and his brain would not co-operate.

"I thought you'd be happy. I didn't plan this. It's not my fault. I bought one of those pregnancy tests, and it turned blue," Karen wept, her voice flooded with concern, "I know we didn't plan this, but, I really hoped you'd be…"

Karen's pain brought Ernie to his senses, and his blank stare transformed into a wicked smile. A wave of true happiness spread through his body, as if a great gift had arrived despite him never asking for it.

"Kazza pet, Ah'm over the moon, like. It's brilliant news," he rejoiced. "Ah'm ganna be a dad. Ah mean, wow. We're ganna be a dad. Ah mean, you know what ah mean. This is more. This is more than ah'd ever hoped for." Ernie picked up Karen in his arms and twirled her around the hall. Then his leg gave way and he landed in a heap on the floor for the third time in as many minutes, but it did not matter, the woman he adored was pregnant with his child. Surely his life could not get better than this.

o o o

The next day a sodden figure leant against the bronze statue of a famous footballer which stood in the middle of Northumberland Street. Northumberland Street was Newcastle's main High Street, and the statue was positioned perfectly to conceal Ernie as he scoped out a lingerie shop. It was a typically unfriendly November day, as he blew into his cupped hands, hopelessly trying to warm them. An icy wind tore through his red Nike tracksuit as he tried to shelter from the hail. Ernie pushed his shivering body closer to the sculpture of "Whor" Jackie Milburn, the legendary 1940's striker, hoping it might save him from the hypothermia that was creeping up on him. Much to Ernie's dismay the statue was freezing too, and the youngster cursed every time his back touched it.

"This is it," he thought. *"This is the last time ah pinch anything."* He remembered the heroic kung fu monk who had inspired his desire to be a better man. *"Ah'm ganna be a dad soon, ah can't be making a living thieving anymore."* Ernie could have turned around and walked away. He could have quit whilst he was ahead, but he made another choice. He felt he had to get Karen something to mark their special occasion. *"Joost one more, that's all"* he told his conscience, as he imagined Karen's cute little bum squeezing into whatever underwear he was about to liberate from the lingerie shop. Ernie did not know what he was going to steal for her, but that was okay. She looked fantastic in anything, and even better in nothing. He was going to be a father. He felt so proud. Six months ago, he had never kissed a girl, and now he was going to have a family of his own. *"Will it be a boy or a girl? Ah hope it gets its' mum's looks."*

Ernie emerged from his fantasy and peered into the lingerie shop. The store manager and a check out girl were trying to calm down an irate customer, who was complaining about the quality of a blow-up doll. The store had a "no return" policy on such items, but the customer did not seem to get the point. Ernie checked his watch. He had only been spying on the shop for ten minutes, but it was so cold. *"Sod it, ma balls are ganna freeze if ah stay here,"* he thought. A moment before he made his move the soft voice of his conscience whispered in his heart.

"Don't do it. It's not right," it said, and Ernie stopped. Perhaps he should walk away.

"Just one more," he told himself, and as the

customer waved the deflated sex aid at the staff, Ernie took his chance and strolled into the shop looking as inconspicuous as he could.

Three minutes later, with two knicker and bra combinations tucked down his boxer shorts, Ernie hobbled away at an even pace. His back straightened and his shoulders relaxed as he felt the pleasure of success course through his body. *"Like taking candy from a barn,"* he thought smugly, but the moment he did, a strong hand landed firmly on his shoulder, sending a shockwave through his body. He knew what had happened and without turning around he made a run for it. More of a hobble than a run, as Ernie was no Carl Lewis and it was icy underfoot. His escape attempt was thwarted by a deft leg sweep from an overzealous store detective. It sent Ernie and his crutches flying, and the young Geordie was kissing pavement before he got two yards. In a flash, the store detective was sitting on top of Ernie, pinning his arm behind his back in an excruciating *Ju Jitsu* armlock. Just Ernie's luck to be collared by a third Dan having a bad day. As his face was pushed into a half-frozen puddle and his tracksuit hungrily soaked up the freezing slush like a sponge, a familiar inner voice spoke familiar words,

"Ah was reet. The good times never last."

What a fool he had been. He had ignored Karen's advice.

"Always, always, *always* scope out any shop for at least half an hour before you whip anything," she had told him. "Then you'll be able to spot if they've got a store detective or not."

Sod's law, this was the first time he had not bothered.

"Damn it!"

Half an hour later a silent, soaking and thoroughly disheartened Ernie was escorted to the local nick. His photograph was taken front and side, and his fingers stained with black ink as they took his prints. One of the policemen then told him to remove his shoes and belt and lead him to a tiny cell whose walls were covered in graffiti. The only piece of furniture was a hard, wooden bench bolted to the wall, which was too short for Ernie to lie down on.

It was a long afternoon with nothing to keep him company but the thoughts in his head. He so wanted to see Karen but could not bring himself to call her. If there was a way he could sort this mess out without having to get her involved, he was going to find it. *"She doesn't need to know what happened today. Not with the baby on the way. She doesn't need the stress,"* he told himself, full of regrets.

The next day Ernie was released without charge.

"But don't go on any holidays abroad. We haven't finished with you, young man," the custody sergeant told him sternly as he handed Ernie back his belt and shoes. Ernie hobbled to Haymarket bus station in the centre of the city with his head hanging and his heart aching. He used the last of his change to buy a ticket for the five-o-three bus to East Shields.

When he got home, he made himself a cup of tea and sat down on his mother's old sofa to think through what had happened. Would the police charge him? Or let him off with a warning? The second possibility did not seem too hopeful. He had been stealing from shops on the High Street for weeks and had a feeling that although the police had released him it was not going to last. What if they found more evidence?

o o o

At eight o'clock that evening Ernie's doorbell rang. Once again, he shot out of the sofa as if he had been electrocuted. *"Ah must get that buzzer fixed, like. It scares the shit out of me every time,"* he thought.

Two police officers were standing at the door.

"What do yoose want now?" Ernie moaned, his heart sinking. "Ah've just come back from the nick, like."

"Ernie Manning?"

"Yes."

"We have CCTV footage of a man matching your description robbing a dozen shops in the city centre over the last few weeks," said Sergeant Simmons, a tough looking copper with a square, stubbled jaw and a nose that had been broken too many times. "You've been a busy boy, haven't you? We need you to come down to the station with us," he insisted. "You're in a lot of trouble young man."

o o o

The magistrate who saw Ernie the following day made it clear he had no chance of bail.

"Bail? And let you out so you can continue your rampage? Not a chance, young man."

Ernie looked to his Legal Aid representative who just shrugged his shoulders. There was no point protesting. Ernie was sent to a remand centre fourteen miles outside East Shields as the police built their case against him. Stubbornly hoping he could still sort this mess out on his own, Ernie was too ashamed to call Karen and tell her what was going on. He had let her down when she needed him the most. The nights were getting darker, as were his days.

CHAPTER 7

Betrayal

Tarquin's eyes rolled upwards into his skull as his body slumped into the racing seat of the Aston Martin. The Fat Man looked over at his son and grinned. It had been most enjoyable to experience a steelier side of Tarquin, but he had no desire to be accidentally shot by his trembling offspring. The Fat Man shook his head. When it came to dealing with his son, shaking his head was becoming a common occurrence. He had been clever enough to evade the police for thirty years, was Tarquin really so naive he thought he could get one over on his old man?

At the next layby, the Fat Man stopped the car, removed the tape from Tarquin's Dictaphone, and tossed the tiny recorder back at the unconscious body still strapped into the passenger seat. Carefully placing the cassette in his jacket pocket he chuckled, reveling in his victory.

"Perhaps I can use it for my memoirs?" he thought and taking a silk handkerchief from his suit jacket pocket, he picked up Tarquin's pistol and locked it in the glove box. It was a tight squeeze with so many unpaid parking tickets sharing the small compartment, but a handgun with his son's fingerprints all over it might prove useful someday. Taking out a silver cigarette case and a matching silver lighter, the Fat Man lit up a Marlboro Red and took a long, deep drag. The lighter had the Chinese characters for 'victory at all cost' engraved onto it. An unnecessary reminder for him to never back down.

"Cigarette?" the Fat Man asked his unconscious son and grunted as no reply came back. As he hit the gas and tore out of the layby Tarquin moaned, and the Fat Man laughed all the way to London.

o o o

Karen and her Aunt Rose sat in the kitchen of the small townhouse in East Shields where they had lived together since they had moved there. The heavy rain pattered hypnotically against the windows of the old house, and the mood inside was even heavier than the rain. Karen was distraught, holding her head in her hands, sobbing uncontrollably, as Rose sat opposite her waiting patiently for Karen to open up.

"I haven't heard a word from Ernie for three days. He's not at home. I've called all the hospitals, I've been to all his hang outs, and I can't find him anywhere. It's like he's vanished. He never goes anywhere without telling me. Something must have happened to him, otherwise he'd have called." Karen's normally carefree face looked drawn, her hair greasy and her eyes bloodshot. "Wouldn't he?" Karen studied her Aunt, hoping to get an answer but fearing what it might be. Rose sat silently for a long time, collecting her thoughts, and then began to speak in a voice that sounded calmer than she felt.

"Karen love, I don't know how to say this," She said, looking down at the napkin she was fingering nervously, still undecided as to what she could tell her niece without making everything much worse. "I know you don't want to hear this, but I've had a bad feeling about Ernie since the day I met him. I know he does his best, and I can see his heart is in the right place, but he doesn't seem like the kind of guy you should be settling down with. He's not the reliable type, if you know what I mean?" she grimaced.

"I'm not stupid," Karen snapped, "I know you've never liked him. I know you think he's not good enough for me, but you're wrong."

"If I am wrong then I am sorry, but I care about you, and I care about your future. Every day since school finished you and Ernie have disappeared to God knows where and I have no idea what you are getting up to. You don't tell me anything anymore, Karen. You come back after midnight, and I can smell beer on you. I'm not stupid either. I was your age once. On top of all that, you haven't done anything about your mechanics training. You two have been fooling around for weeks, but you can't do that forever, you're an adult now. I want you to be with someone who can support you, someone who isn't a bad influence, or disappears on a whim." Rose knew this was not going to go well.

"I know we've not been taking life as seriously as we should, but it's only been a few weeks. We had to let off some steam after the exams. Surely you can understand that? Ernie isn't perfect, but I love him. I love him more than anyone. Surely that's enough?" Karen replied as she blew her nose into one of Ernie's handkerchiefs.

"I know what it's like to be in love, Karen. I really do," Rose continued, "But I'm not sure love is always enough. We do stupid things when we are young, we have strange ideas about life. I'm the closest thing you have to a parent, and I'd be letting you down if I didn't tell you what I think. I am not going to force you to do anything, but I can't sit back and watch you ruin your life without saying anything either. Ernie's the first guy you've fallen for, and he won't be the last."

Karen's tears had dried and been replace by a frustrated glare.

"I remember the first time I got my heart broken. It was awful. I thought my world had collapsed and I would never be happy again, but I was. People get over their disappointments Karen, and so will you."

"You don't know that he doesn't want to be with me," Karen cried out. Aunt Rose's words were the last thing she wanted to hear, yet she knew there was something to them. She shivered, wondering if she had got Ernie wrong. Maybe he really had done a runner? He had been so distant when she had told him about the pregnancy, and the faraway look in his eyes had unnerved her. Perhaps he was not the guy she thought he was? "No, way," Karen whispered under her breath, and then raised her voice. "I'm not stupid, and I have not got Ernie wrong."

"I hope so. I truly want the best for you, Karen," Aunt Rose replied.

"But what if you don't know what that is? What if me and Ernie can work? Perhaps we don't have to be cardboard cut outs of the perfect people to be happy? I *really* know him. You don't. No, something bad must have happened. It must have," Karen composed herself, when it would have felt more natural to throw a plate at her Aunt's head. Aunt Rose heard Karen's words, but she did not listen to them. She could not. She had made up her mind weeks before, and Ernie's absence was confirmation of what a rat he was.

"The first is the most difficult to let go of," Rose continued, "listen, you have your whole life ahead of you, and you have a lot going for you. I don't really know how to say this, but I'm going to say it anyway. He's not a catch," Aunt Rose winced as the words came out, then held her breath.

"You don't know what you are talking about," Karen erupted, shaking with rage. "Ernie Manning is the kindest, most thoughtful guy I've ever met. I would marry him in a heartbeat. He's different to other guys. I know you don't see it, but I do." Karen's lower lip started to shake, and she broke down in tears once more. Rose put a hand on Karen's shoulder.

"I'm sorry love, I should not have said that. I know I don't know him the way you do. I'm just worried."

"So, what could have happened to him?"

"I don't know, but perhaps he got scared. For some reason he felt he had to disappear. If he'd hurt himself we'd know about it. Heaven forbid, if something worse had happened to him, I'm sure we would have heard about that too. But nothing, not a word. It doesn't make any sense, unless," her eyes bore into Karen. "Did you two have a fight? Did something happen that might have scared him off?"

Karen remembered Ernie's reaction when she had told him she was pregnant.

"I've got to tell her," she thought.

"I'm going to have a baby, Aunt Rose, Ernie's baby. I'm pregnant."

"Oh, my dear girl, I had no idea."

Karen nodded.

"I was going to tell you, but I thought you'd be angry. I thought if me and Ernie could work something out, some way to make a living, then I could tell you."

"Oh Karen. I'm not the kind of person who ditches the people I love because they're having a hard time. I'll support you as best I can, no matter what happens. I'm with you one hundred percent." Rose put down the napkin and hugged Karen tightly. For the first time in days, Karen relaxed. Finally, Rose was on her side.

"I took a test, twice. I bought them kit at the chemist, and they went blue both times."

"Oh Karen, that explains it all. He did get scared."

"Aunt Rose, come on. You said you were going to support me, and that is not supporting me."

"I'm sorry," offered Rose, "I'm not getting any

younger, and it's not so easy for old people like me who are getting long in the tooth. We aren't so good at understanding the youth of today," she smiled at Karen, who allowed herself half a smile back at her Aunt.

"I know. I know, but as you said yourself. I'm an adult now. Ernie was shocked when I told him, but he came around to the idea. Then he seemed really excited about it. He grabbed me and twirled me round the room," Karen said, trying to convince herself more than Aunt Rose.

"You know his father left his mother before Ernie was born, don't you? Could he not have got scared and done the same as his old man?" Rose regretting her words before they had come out.

"So much for supporting me! I don't want to hear any more about him deserting me. Ernie would never do that. I am sure of it. Never!" Karen shouted, then ran upstairs to her room, slamming the door behind her.

Rose sat staring at the space where Karen had been sitting. It was not easy being a step-parent. Then she sighed, picked up and then folded the blue napkin she had been playing with, and got up to peel some potatoes for supper.

o o o

An hour later, as Rose stood next to the cooker stirring her vegetable stew, the phone in the kitchen rang. Rose picked it up cautiously.

"Hello."

"Hello, Rose, it's Ernie here," came a faint voice on the crackly line.

"Ernie, my goodness, where are you? Are you okay?" she asked in a hushed voice.

"Not really. Ah haven't got long enough to explain, like. Ah really need to talk to Karen."

"Ernie, where have you been for the last three days? We've been worried sick."

"Ah'm in the nick, ah've been done for shoplifting. It looks like ah'm ganna be inside for a while. Can ah speak to Karen now?"

Rose paused, holding the receiver to her chest. After a long time she slowly moved it back to her ear, and spoke a sentence she would never have wanted to say.

"No Ernie, you can't. She's too good for you, and I think you know that. Do you really think you can be a father when you can't stay out of trouble yourself? If you've got an ounce of decency in you, you'll walk away from her and the baby. If you love them, you will walk away. I'm sorry Ernie, I am sorry."

Before Ernie could reply Rose hung up the receiver and unplugged the phone from the wall. A pained expression contorted her otherwise friendly face, and she bit her lip as if to punish herself for what she had just done.

o o o

"Ah, Tarquin how's the chin?" the Fat Man taunted with a glint in his eye. Tarquin touched his jaw tentatively. It hurt, but as he moved it from side to side, he was relieved to discover it was not broken. He had been unconscious for an hour or so, which was more than enough time for the Fat Man to have killed him and disposed of his body. Yet here he was alive and kicking. Trying to blackmail the Fat Man and living to tell the tale was unheard of, and anyone else but Tarquin would be six feet under by now. Being the Fat Man's only son had undoubtedly saved his life. Mind you, he should not count his chickens just yet, as he had no idea what his father had planned for him.

Sometime later the Fat Man pulled to a halt in front of Tarquin's flat in central London. Tarquin scrambled out of the Aston, stumbling as he trotted away from his insane father without saying a word. He was so relieved to be out of the car he wanted to break into a run but chose to retain whatever semblance of dignity he had left.

"Ice that chin when you get home, you don't

want to look like a hamster for the rest of the week," the Fat Man instructed. Tarquin did not want to turn around, but forced himself, out of habit rather than courtesy.

"Sure, okay, bye," he mumbled.

"I'll be in touch," his father said nonchalantly, as if it had been just another day in the office. Then he shifted the Aston into first gear and shot off into the traffic, going nowhere in particular at breakneck speed.

o o o

Now he was alone the Fat Man's mind drifted back over twenty years, caught up in a memory he did not want to re-live, but could not help himself from doing so.

"*Damn you John Malone...*

It was the summer of 1961. Elvis Presley's 'Surrender' topped the charts, and John F. Kennedy and Nikita Krushchev nearly nuked all life on earth. On top of all this Nigel Kensington, later to be known as the Fat Man, was furious. No, he was not furious. He was a raging tempest of hate. He was ready to hurt, to kill, anything to sate his anger, and it was not because of the prospect of nuclear war. Sophie had betrayed him in the worst possible way, with John Malone, his best friend of all people. They had led Nigel a sorry dance and he had not yet had the pleasure of strangling them both with his bare hands.

Now the twenty-something Nigel was miles away from the treacherous lovebirds, driving like a man possessed. He had lost the only thing he truly loved, and with her life had lost all meaning.

Nought to 60 in five seconds. Four and a half if he redlined it.

Any desire to drive in a way that might keep him or other drivers in one piece was gone. No part of him cared whether he lived or died.

"Damn you both," he cursed, blinded by emotion and stunned by his loss. As Nigel exited a sharp corner somewhere between Eastleigh and Winchester, something happened that would change his life forever. Ten yards in front of him a small, barefooted girl was standing in the middle of the road. She could not have been more than eleven years old. She had red hair and pigtails and was wearing a handmade white dress which was soaking wet and looked like it came from Victorian times. Nigel's reactions were fast, and his thick racing tires scorched the asphalt as he slammed on the brakes. At that speed he could not hope to control the bright yellow MGBG he had bought only weeks before. The car started to skid to the left and then the right, twisting and slipping like a cut eel. For a

split second he had a choice. Hit the girl or plough into the huge oak tree to her right. He chose the tree.

Crunch.

Sixty to nought in zero seconds.

Nigel's soul was slammed into darkness.
Time stood still. Nothing. Black. Empty. Peaceful. No suffering. No pain.
He could have stayed there forever.
He wanted to stay there forever.

Sometime later a man pulled up in a grey Renault 5. He got out of his car, fearing what he might find, and rushed over to the crumpled wreck that had been Nigel's pride and joy.
Kevin's voice pierced the emptiness.
"Are you all right mate?" he asked, leaning over Nigel to turn off the ignition.
"Ugh," Nigel groaned as the man touched his shoulder, stealing him away from the peaceful place. When Nigel opened his eyes, he was met with a foggy blur. "Where am I?" He asked, and then images of the barefooted girl, the Victorian dress, the tree, and that bastard John Malone engulfed his mind. "Where am I? Ugh," he grunted, it was so hard to think. The fog faded

a little and he could see he was still in his car, trapped. The trunk of a huge oak tree stood only inches from his nose, and his oversized body was bent over the steering wheel, hugging it to his chest. Nigel's racing harness was the only thing that had saved him from losing a head-butting competition with the tree, and every part of his body hurt. It felt like an ice pick had been driven into his eye, and a ghastly throb from the depths of his skull made him groan in pain every time he breathed.

"Arrgh."
"Don't try to get up, mate. I'll get help. Stay here," the man told him.

"No. Arrgh." Another sharp pain shot through Nigel's arm. "Pull me out of this bloody thing before it explodes!" he ordered. The Good Samaritan pulled the driver's door as hard as he could, but it would not open. So, he kicked it and tried again. It opened. He lent in and undid the driver's seatbelt, and then struggled to pull the huge man out of his concertinaed car. The man collapsed onto the ground. "Damn it!" he cursed, pulling himself onto his feet, and steadying himself on the bonnet of his car. Then Nigel stumbled and fell again. "It takes more than a car crash to keep me down," he seethed at no-one in particular, once more pulling himself to his feet. He clumsily patted down his smoking pin-striped suit, with a vacant expression on his face. "What the hell is that?" he exclaimed, as he

noticed a shard of glass sticking out of his arm. Touching it with his stubby fingertips, as if to check that he was not imagining it, he gasped. He did not like the look of that glass. "What the hell happened to me?" he boomed in pain, unable to ignore the dark, uncontrollable rage welling up inside him.

"You've had quite a shock," the man told him, trying to keep calm. "It's glass, from the windscreen. Whatever you do don't touch it. Winchester hospital's only ten miles away. I'll get you an ambulance. Give me five minutes, there's a phone box up the road. I'll drive there, okay?"

"What? Where? Who are you? Why did you crash into my car?" the Fat Man blustered.

"It's alright. Just sit down over here, gently does it, away from the car. By the way, my name's Kevin." The man reassured him, putting a friendly hand on the Fat Man's shoulders.

Thump.

Before he could drive to the phone box, Kevin Stainforth, accounting assistant for Crawley Council, had been thrown to the ground and was being savagely kicked and punched by the very man he had tried to help.

"I'll teach you, John Malone, I'll teach you for

screwing my fiancé, you bastard. I'll teach you for ruining my life," Nigel screamed as he laid into his rescuer, confused and hurt, the pain in his arm making him wild with anger. Kevin had no chance against the bull elephant who had taken him by surprise.

It was only when Kevin's face was bloodied, his nose and ribs smashed to pieces, and he was lying on the ground unconscious, that Nigel finally stopped. "I hope you rot in hell John Malone," he panted, sweat seeping into his still smoldering clothes. Finally, he leaned back against the bonnet of his car, exhausted.

o o o

That afternoon, Nigel staggered up the front steps of his country home. The glass still wedged in his shoulder, and blood still oozing from the wound. Once inside, he went to his drawing room, poured himself a large whiskey, knocking it back in one gulp.

"Bloody hell," he muttered and poured himself another. He looked around and saw a small, embroidered tablecloth on one of the coffee tables. He grabbed the corner of it and pulled hard. The cloth came free with a swish, crystal smashed, and two plates clattered on the floor. Nigel then wrapped the tablecloth around the glass in his arm and with one swift movement he ripped it out. "Bollocks," he

screamed. The gash of muscle, blood and bone that remained was too much for him and he promptly fainted, crashing to the floor.

When Nigel came to, his lower lip was stuck to the carpet with dried spittle and his head was thumping. Blinking his eyes, he picked himself off the floor and stumbled towards a telephone sitting on the windowsill. Looking out of the window he could see a grey Renault 5 standing in the driveway.

"Whose bloody car is that?" he thought, as he dialed a number he knew by heart.

"Mickey," Nigel growled, "I need you to pick my car up. I've had a little accident."

"Sure Boss," the Bouncer replied, his Cockney accent showing a hint of concern, "are you okay?"

"I'm alright. It's somewhere on the little B-road between Winchester and Eastleigh, you know the one?"

"I know it. I'll come over and get your keys?"

"No. No need for keys. Take a pick up and a crane."

"Uh, okay, Boss."

"There's probably still a guy there, maybe unconscious. He's had a bit of a going over. Get him to the hospital, and make sure he's looked after, but don't tell him who you are, alright?"

"Understood."

"And Mickey, get there as quickly as you can."

The Fat Man slammed the receiver down hard and the phone fell to the floor with a desperate ring. He picked up the whiskey glass lying next to him, refilled it, and threw it down his throat in one gulp. "Medicinal purposes," he told himself. Images of the crash flashed through his mind, and as did the beating he had dished out to the stranger. "Poor sod," Nigel muttered, as he poured himself another whiskey, "wrong guy, wrong place, wrong time."

CHAPTER 8

Heart break

A week had passed, and Karen had still heard nothing from Ernie. As they had done every evening since Ernie had disappeared, she and Aunt Rose sat in the kitchen together, Karen with her head in her hands and Rose fidgeting with the same blue napkin. Tonight, they said little to each other, choosing instead to grind over different scenarios in their heads. Karen battled with two horribly unpleasant possibilities. The first was that something terrible had befallen Ernie and she would never see him again. The Second was that nothing terrible had happened, but he never wanted to see her again. Rose on the other hand was torn between the guilt of seeing Karen in pain, and the relief that her niece might be free of a millstone that had hung around her neck all summer.

"Men can be so strange," said Rose, feeling a need to break the uncomfortable silence. "Sometimes they need a bit of time to get used to a situation, and sometimes they run. His Dad did the same…"

"Not again," Karen interrupted angrily. "You were going on about this last night, and the night before and the night before that. We still don't know what's happened to him. I wish you would just listen to me."

"I'm sorry Karen, I never learn do I?"

"Not really," Karen replied, looking out of the window with a stubborn expression. "By the way, when Ernie comes back, we're going to move in together. We're going to get a little flat and make a family of our own. I'm a grown up now," she declared, waiting to see what reaction she had provoked.

"Okay, yes, I think you're right," replied Rose much to Karen's dismay. "I don't want to see you go, but maybe you should."

Karen took a deep breath.

"You've always been kind to me, and if you hadn't taken me in I'd have ended up in some horrible orphanage, hating it. But you're probably right. I do need to move out. I can't rely on you for everything."

Rose frowned.

"Yes, I think I am right. It probably isn't good for

you to live with me at the moment."

"Where would I go? I don't have anyone except for you and Ernie," Karen paused, her heart breaking as she spoke. "I mean, I don't have anyone except for you. I feel so lost." Tears of loneliness overtook Karen once more, and Rose put a comforting hand on Karen's. Rose hated lying to her niece, but what other choice did she have? If she told her where Ernie was, Karen would be hitchhiking to the remand centre before Rose had finished her sentence, and it probably would not be long before Ernie was knocking on her front door. Getting Karen out of East Shields, at least for a while, was the only option to keep her and Ernie apart.

"Listen Karen, hear me out. I know a man. He lives in Scotland and he is a true gentleman. His name is Rex. He lives in a big white house near Inverness, with lots of space. Hanging around Newcastle twiddling your thumbs, thinking about what has happened isn't going to do you or the baby any good. It's going to drive you and me mad. Take some time to get away from all this. Somewhere you can collect your thoughts and get your strength back. When you come back, I can look after the little one if you still want to do your mechanics training? But that doesn't start until November."

"Tell me more about this guy, Rex," asked Karen drying her tears with her hand.

"Well, he's a very nice man. He was in the army

and then he went into business, but he's been living on his own in this big house for many years. It's a lovely house on the top of a hill, next to a wood, looking down on a river. His son, Raymond, your mother and me were inseparable when we were children. We spent most of our time at Raymond's house, playing in the garden, climbing trees, you know? Kid's stuff. Raymond emigrated to New Zealand twenty years ago, but Rex and I have kept in touch. Rex is a gourmet cook and he loves the outdoor life. Perhaps you could stay with him for a while? I know he could do with the company."

Karen felt strangely drawn to this man she had never met.

"It sounds kind of nice."

"I haven't spoken to him for a couple of years, but I could ring him up, and ask?" Rose suggested gently, the blue napkin still clasped in her fingers.

"But what about Ernie? I *need* to find him. I can't go and live somewhere else, what if he comes back?"

"I know pet, but he'll find you when he's ready. Right now, the best thing is for you to gather your strength. It'll only be for a few weeks, and once Ernie comes around to the idea of being a father, perhaps he'll come back? If he comes knocking on the door, I'll tell him where you are." Rose looked away from Karen full of shame.

"No-one deserves to start out in life with a loser like Ernie Manning," she told herself with a heavy heart.

Had Karen been her usual self she would have smelled a rat, but she had hardly slept for days, and her head was full of dread and heartache. Besides, there was something comforting about the idea of spending time with one of her mother's old friends. Aunt Rose had never talked about Rex, yet something about his name piqued Karen's curiosity. Going to Inverness had to be better than waiting for Ernie to muster up the courage to contact her.

o o o

It had rained non-stop for a week, and Karen had heard every drop patter down on the skylight in her room as she lay in bed thinking about Ernie. As she got up and packed the last of her clothes into an old brown suitcase, she felt exhausted, ten years older than her years. Picking up a photograph of her and Ernie in happier times she paused, unsure of what to do with it. It had stood on her bedside table since they had been away to Seahouses a few weeks before. That short holiday had been the happiest two days of her life.

"I should throw this in the bin," thought Karen,

but as she looked closer at the two of them, arm in arm, with wide grins and sparkling eyes, she knew she could not give up on him. Holding the photograph to her chest, the memories of Ernie whisking her away for that romantic trip, flooded back to her. They had stayed in a dodgy bed and breakfast and he had made her laugh non-stop. Karen remembered the grumpy, old lady who ran the bed and breakfast. She was not used to having two seventeen-year-old's keeping her up all night. To top it off, Ernie had turned up for breakfast dressed in Elton John glasses, an afro-wig and a pink suit Karen had bought him from a charity shop. The old lady's sense of humour was non-existent, and before they had finished breakfast, she had told them to leave.

Karen had wanted to let down her car tyres but Ernie had stopped her.

"Let bygones be bygones, pet," he had told her, "poor lady, she doesn't know how to have fun. Let's not be mean to her just because she doesn't understand us, like."

That was the kind of guy Ernie was, and that was what she wanted to remember. Later that morning an American tourist had taken their photo, as they giggled happily at the foot of a sycamore tree in the park. They looked so happy.

Karen laid the photo on top of her clothes,

kissed two of her fingers and placed them gently on the glass. She knew she could decide how to approach this heartbreaking event. She could resent Ernie, the easiest choice, or know that sometimes people let you down and it is not their fault. The second choice was the hardest to make but it was the wisest and the one she chose.

"I hope you're okay, Ernie, wherever you are," she whispered and rested her hand on her tummy. For the first time in Karen's life she had been happy, and it was because of a skinny, redhead with bucked teeth who had opened her heart. Now he was gone, leaving her full of regrets and an unborn child in her womb. Why was life so cruel? Why had it dealt her such shitty cards? She remembered lying on the bonnet of the red Ford Escort at St. Mary's Island, when Ernie had told her that life was like a poker game. If life was a poker game, she was slap bang in the middle of a losing streak, in debt to some nasty loan sharks and staring into the abyss. Right now, she did not feel like playing poker at all, but play she must.

A few months earlier, Karen would have been consumed with rage if she had fallen pregnant and her lover had disappeared, but now she was a different person. She had tasted the delight of true love and that delight had strengthened her beyond measure. It had soothed the anger that had lived inside her for as long as she could remember. An anger that was fueled by her the loss of her mother, violent stepfathers and a deep sense of injustice. Her first reaction had always been to hit out. Yet strangely, in the midst of these dark times, Karen found that her love did not turn to hate but deepened instead.

Downstairs the phone rang, and Aunt Rose trotted back to the kitchen, looking apprehensively over her shoulder. Picking up the receiver she whispered,

"Five, five, three, two, one, seven. Who's speaking, please?"

Ernie's ten pence piece fell into the remand centre payphone.

"Hello, Rose, it's Ernie. Please don't hang up. Will you let me talk to Karen, like? Ah need to talk to her, to give us a chance to sort things out. They only give us one call a week. Please?" Ernie pleaded.

"Ernie, I'm sorry. I've told her where you are, and she doesn't want to talk to you. She doesn't want you in her life. I'm sorry, Ernie, but that's the way it is," Rose lied, her voice trembling.

"Ah don't believe you. Ah want to hear *her* say it. Ah want to hear it from Karen," he pressed, looking nervously behind for the guard who would soon force him to hang up.

"She's right here Ernie, sitting next to me. She

says she doesn't want to speak to you," Rose lied again.

"Please Rose, give me a minute. Can't you persuade her, like?"

"That's it Manning, your time's up," a guard told him, as he pulled Ernie away from the payphone. Then the beeps bleeped and the line went dead. Rose put down the receiver and quietly unplugged the phone again.

"It's time to go Karen," she shouted from the kitchen, holding back her tears. "I'll come and help you with your suitcase."

Karen was already halfway down the stairs.

"I'm fine, it's not heavy," she insisted.

"Karen, you mustn't carry things in your condition. When are you going to learn to look after yourself?"

"Who was that on the phone?" Karen asked, dragging her suitcase into the kitchen.

"Oh, an old friend of mine, someone I didn't expect to hear from. She's going to call back later."

"You look like you've seen a ghost," Karen remarked suspiciously.

"Yes, it does feel a bit like that. I didn't expect to hear from her. It brought back a lot of old memories." Rose felt horrible. She could hear the desperation in Ernie's voice, and wondered if she was doing the right thing.

"But that is not my concern," she reassured herself, *"I have to protect my niece. The niece who got herself banged up by some seventeen-year-old idiot who's not capable of tying his own shoelaces, let alone bringing up a family."* This mess had happened on Rose's watch, and she was going to do her best to tidy it up, even if that meant lying to the person she loved more than anyone. *"Family is family"*, she told herself. It was better that Ernie and Karen never set eyes on each other ever again.

Ernie shrugged off the guard's hand as he hobbled back to his cell thinking,

"The good times never last." Of course, his few months of happiness had been too good to be true. He had known it all along. *"Why would Karen fall for a loser like me? Rose is right, ah'd only cause them pain. Ah'm not cut oot to be a dad, like."* People were not in the habit of giving out jobs to teenage criminals, and Ernie's chances of supporting a family had disappeared the instant the store detective had collared him.

A month after his arrest, Ernie was handcuffed and driven to Heaton High Court in the back of a police van. The judge found him guilty of seventeen counts of shoplifting and sentenced him to six months in a young offenders' institute a few miles south of Durham. Ernie was distraught. It was the end of the road for the young couple. Paradise was well and truly lost.

o o o

Kevin the Accounting Assistant for Crawley County Council was still unconscious when the Bouncer found him lying next to the remains of Nigel's car. The huge tattooed arms of Mickey the 'Bouncer' picked him up with ease. He then put him in the cab of his lorry and drove to Eastleigh Green hospital. Pulling into a deserted parking lot at the back of the hospital, the Bouncer could see a couple of ambulances, but no-one else around. With the unconscious man in his arms he kicked open a scruffy looking side door, entering what looked like the hospital's waste disposal unit. The Bouncer skillfully avoided the porters and nurses he encountered, finding his way to a deserted corridor where he spotted an empty hospital trolley. With great care laid Kevin on the trolley.

"Where am I?" Kevin murmured, starting to come to. The Bouncer put a huge hand over Kevin's face and whispered kindly.

"Wait for the doctor. He won't be long. You're going to be okay." He pushed the trolley through the double doors leading into the brightly lit reception area. There it slowly came to a halt right in front of the charge nurse's desk. The Bouncer was already marching back the way he had come, when Kevin was discovered. He jumped into the cab of his lorry and sped back to the

scene of the crash. There he winched what was left of his boss's wreck onto the back of his lorry and drove back to London.

Kevin was rushed into one of the operating rooms where, against the odds, the surgeons saved his life. He would never be quite the same again.

CHAPTER 9

Rex

Up until that fateful day, Kevin had been charmed with good fortune. His childhood had been happy, with his parents giving him all the opportunities they could. He had taken the middle-class route from an all-boys grammar school to reading accounting at Cardiff. It was there, on the vibrant University campus, that he had met the love of his life, Brenda, and he had never looked back.

Brenda was in her second year, studying statistics and further mathematics. She would never have been be classed as a heart stopper but was outrageously intelligent, steaming towards a double first when Kevin first met her at the chess club. Kevin admired intelligent women, and there was something about Brenda's thick rimmed spectacles and bowl haircut that drove him wild. He had decided on a whim to have a look at the chess club, and the first person he saw was Brenda. Over the next ten minutes he had watched her checkmate two of the finest players in the club, and in that instant, he knew he had found the love of his life. She was the first woman he had ever dated, but they had so much in common he found it easy to spend time with her. Whenever they talked statistics or sat down with two gin and tonics and a chess board, Kevin could not keep his hands off her, and Brenda was not complaining.

A year later they moved into a small flat together, and three years after that they were married. Kevin and Brenda Stainforth then bought a little house on the outskirts of Cambridge, which they shared with two black Labradors and a cat called Percival. Kevin worked as a junior accountant and Brenda as a part time librarian. She spent her free time writing a four hundred-thousand-word epic titled,

"Check-mate comrade: Ruthless Russian chess battles of the seventies".

They lived in a quiet village which had a sleepy pub, a village store and a Post Office that closed at two in the afternoon. The raucous parties that might have shattered the triple-glazed serenity of their new home were absent, and they liked it that way. It was by no means an exhilarating life, but they were content. Their neighbours too were keen to maintain a healthy distance. Perhaps a nod might be exchanged across the isle of the village store, but nothing more. From behind the safety of his picket fence, Kevin would sometimes comment on the tyre trims of his neighbour's new Mitsubishi Shogun, but anything more than that was overstepping the boundaries of common decency. Forming friendships could take years.

Every Sunday Kevin would spend a couple of hours in his driveway polishing his grey Renault 5, and Brenda would walk the dogs come rain or shine. It was good to have routine. The only exciting thing that happened in their first few years in Cambridgeshire, involved a pair of fluffy handcuffs Brenda had bought Kevin for Valentine's Day. They were a touch risqué, but why not experiment a little? Although they never discussed their sex life directly, both of them felt like spicing things up a bit. Alas, the excitement of the handcuffs was short lived, following an embarrassing episode with some whipped cream and the fire brigade. So much for excitement! Life rolled on from one day to the next without very much happening at all. If things got boring, they redecorated another room. Kevin was so grateful for DIY shows, which may very well have saved more marriages than Relate. They could both have lived like this for the rest of their days, but as is so often the case life had other plans.

o o o

In 1961 the summer came around as it had done so the year before and the year before that. The Beetles had finished recording 'If You Love Me Baby' and Rod Laver had won Wimbledon. However, in those days Kevin had no time for such trivial matters. He was up to his ears in audits and had been working flat out for eight weeks to get through the backlog. To confound his frustration, he had been tormented by the unusually hot weather that everyone else in Britain was basking in.

It was a sweltering Tuesday when Kevin finally finished the last of his audits.

"Time to take a drive and treat myself to lunch and a quiet pint somewhere," he thought to himself. Hardly able to contain his euphoria, he skipped out of the office and into his Renault 5, started the ignition and pulled away. Not one for speed, he cautiously navigated his car through the winding lanes, rarely shifting above third gear. He passed hedgerows so tall they met at the top, taking time to admire the countryside that had evaded him for the last two months. Every so often Kevin would slow down to a crawl to enjoy the fields of wheat, or ancient oak and

beech copses that populated this part of the country. England truly was a green and pleasant land. "Ah, the open road. This is the life," he thought, as he pressed play on his car stereo and let the uplifting sounds of Vivaldi brighten his mood a little more. Perhaps it was worth working sixteen-hour days, just to have the experience of not having to do it anymore?

Kevin drove into a forested area, keeping his speed to a sensible pace. The forest canopy kept out most of the sunlight, giving it a feeling of dusk even though it was the early afternoon.

"Something's wrong," he thought, as a familiar feeling in his gut arrived out of nowhere. Fifty yards ahead of Kevin was an oddly parked car on the grassy verge. Squinting his eyes, he could see smoke billowing from the bonnet, and for a brief moment he could have sworn he saw a little girl in a white dress standing next to the crumpled wreck.

"Is that an angel?" he asked himself. However, when he got closer no one was there. "Oh no, not good," he whispered to himself. He could see a man trapped inside the car and the man was not moving. He was bald, large framed and blood was pouring his shoulder. His body was pushed up against the steering wheel. He seemed to be unconscious. Kevin stopped the Renault and rushed to the aid of the driver.

"Are you all right mate?" Kevin asked, as he

touched the bald man's good shoulder.

"Ugh," the man grunted as Kevin leaned over him to turn off the ignition.

"Thank God, he's alive," thought Kevin.

"Where am I? Where am I? Ugh," the bald man grunted again.

"Don't try to get up, mate. I'll get help. Stay here," said Kevin, turning to run back to his car.

"No. Arrgh. Pull me out of this bloody thing before it explodes!" the bald man exploded, clearly in a great deal of pain. Kevin found it was hard to understand what he was saying, as his face was so contorted. Kevin was torn between the man's insistence and knowing it would be better to get him an ambulance.

"If this car blows up then no-body can save him," he decided and then tried to open the driver's door. Kevin pulled the door as hard as he could, but it would not budge. So, he kicked it and tried again.

"Thank goodness," he thought as the driver's door came open. He lent in and unbuckled the huge man's seatbelt. It was not an easy task to pull the driver out "You weigh a tonne," Kevin wanted to say, but held himself back. There was something intimidating about this man, even though he was half unconscious.

Kevin finally managed to pull the man's bloated body out of the car, where he stumbled and fell to the *ground.*

Kevin heard him swear as he slowly picked himself up. "Is this guy indestructible?" Kevin wondered. The big man steadied himself on the bonnet of his car but stumbled and fell again. "Arrgh." Rather than give up, he seemed to go into himself, gathering whatever strength he still had. "It takes more than a car crash to keep me down," he seethed in pain, pulling himself to his feet. He then clumsily patted down his smoking pin-striped suit, a vacant expression on his face.

"This man's a tough hombre," thought Kevin, wishing he had already called an ambulance.

"What the hell is that?" the bald man gasped, as he spotted a shard of glass sticking out of his shoulder. "what the hell happened to me?"

"You've had quite a shock," Kevin told him, backing away from the bald man's anger. "It's glass, from the windscreen. Whatever you do don't touch it. Winchester hospital's only ten miles away. I'll get you an ambulance. Give me five minutes, there's a phone box up the road. I'll drive there, okay?"

Thump.

o   o   o

First and foremost, Rex was a distinguished man whose commanding presence would fill a room without him needing to say a word. His back was straight, and he moved deliberately and with a certain grace. Those who knew him well loved him deeply, and those who did not showed him a respect that they somehow sensed he deserved. At eighty-two his body was old, but his spirit was still young, and his long limbs still possessing the strength of a younger man, although not too much younger. Rex invariably dressed in a tweed suit, collared shirt and an old school tie. He spoke deliberately in a deep, warm voice which sounded like velvet bells ringing on a Sunday. The depth of his integrity kept bad people at bay and drew in those whose hearts were full of laughter. Although he did not relish getting old, he accepted it, using it as an excuse to do whatever he wanted. Whether he was threatening to release mice at his nephew's wedding reception, or flirting with an uptight pensioner who worked in a tea shop, he was never far from laughter or mischief. He was a true social liability, and his age and bearing made him invincible. He did not suffer fools gladly and caused chaos wherever he went, and Karen was taken by him from the first moment they met.

"I used to be the second most attractive man in London, you know?" Rex had joked in a distinguished, upper class accent, as he shook her hand on their first meeting. "After Prince Philip. But of course, I've aged a lot better than him," he winked, and Karen laughed. Rex was old school and loved his routine. Every day from around three o'clock in the afternoon he would start on the gin and tonics. "Is that the time?" he would say, aghast, well within earshot of Karen. "Already a quarter past three and my glass is empty, that won't do." Then Karen would make him a gin and tonic with a generous helping of gin, and as much ice as she could fit in the glass. Rex's home was a time capsule in itself. It was full of old, interesting artefacts gathered over lifetimes of adventure and conquest. The severed heads of now rare or extinct animals were dotted around various rooms. Shot in an age where there was still some skill and danger in culling wildlife, which was at that time abundant. A brace of pheasants hung from an old steel hook in one corner of the kitchen, and a throng of antique cookbooks lined the dark pine bookshelves. Rex's velvet sofas and *chaise longs* were upholstered with royal greens and regal blues. There was not a piece of furniture in the house that was not a hundred years old, and the kitchen smelt of game birds, dust and magic. Rex was never happier than when he was enjoying a good conversation in good company or digging his vegetable garden alone. Mud was ever present on his green Wellington boots which stood guard by the back door, ready for their next foray into the artichoke patch.

Most afternoons Karen and Rex would go for a walk together. The distance they covered was not great, but the time they took to do so was. Rex loved to tell Karen stories of the adventures his son Raymond, Aunt Rose and her mother had got up to as children. Raymond was the eldest of the three, but it was Karen's mother who lead this band of friends astray.

"They were always getting themselves into some sort of trouble or other," laughed Rex. "I think I must have been in the headmistress' office more than all the other parents combined."

Karen had an old photograph of her and her mother on holiday in Blackpool, and the fading memories of their time together, but she felt she knew so little about her. Rose had spoken about her sometimes but was not able to bring any of her stories to life. It was incredible to hear what she had been like from a man who had watched her grow up. Karen had never understood why she had rebelled against everything she could, or why she just had to dress differently to everyone else at school. "Your mother put the 'R' into rebel. She just hated being told what do to. Always had to plough her own furrow and the world was a better place for it. I've never met a gutsier woman in my life. Gosh, I remember she sorted out one of the older boys at school. He was bullying someone, and your mother could stand for that. She stamped on his foot so hard it broke his toe and then grabbed him by the ear and gave him hell. I don't think that bully ever hurt anyone again. At least not when she was around."

Karen smiled from the depths of her soul. Her life was starting to make sense. "She was a very pretty girl, but a tom boy through and through, a bit like someone else I know," he winked. "She rebelled against her parents whenever she got the chance. You know," Rex chuckled, "when she was fifteen, she enrolled herself in judo classes. In those days, judo classes were not something that a respectable young woman was supposed to do. Your grandparents hit the roof and banned her from the classes, but she wouldn't give them up. She snuck out of her bedroom window to go and train with all these sweaty men, learning choke holds and how to throw people over her shoulder. Then she would sneak back through her window, and they were none the wiser," Rex's chest puffed up and a look of pride spread across his face. "We didn't win the war by following rules, you know? It was only when she started winning competitions against boys a year or two older than her, that they grudgingly accepted her new hobby and let her train."

"That explains a lot," Karen laughed. "I don't feel nearly as weird now. It's in my genes!"

"Yes, my dear, you certainly aren't a huge fan of being told what to do," Rex chuckled again. Then his mood became more serious. "Of course, all that was before she got ill. That illness really took it out of her. It beat her down. I've never seen anyone change so much in my life." Rex put his hand on Karen's shoulder.

"I'm so sad I never got to experience her as herself. I just remember visits to the hospital and her staring into space, sometimes not even knowing who I was. I mean, we had some good times, but she was sick so much. She was never anything like what you are telling me now. That was gone and now she's dead."

"Well, my Dear, she lives on in you. That's for certain."

It was rare for a city girl to adapt to outdoor life so quickly, but Karen took to it like a duck to water. Rex's home was quiet, and any sounds she did hear came from animals, or trees, or the rain. The Highlands possessed a rugged beauty that enchanted her, and she blossomed in its wild embrace. On rainy days, Karen would sit in an old rocking chair in Rex's drawing room, staring out of the window at the heather clad hills behind his house, enjoying her quiet place where her thoughts and fears no longer touched her. She so enjoyed staring at the scenery, it was so different to East Shields. The wind battered heather wound itself into tangled, snakelike masses, covering the hillsides and stretching as far as the eye could see. Unlike the stringy toughness of the heather, the mosses and lichens that bedded down the grassland around Rex's home felt soft to the touch. When Karen walked, she liked to feel their bounce underfoot, as they propelled her on her way. Stags and hinds, foxes, hares, partridge and adders, became a part of her life. She learned to approach them from downwind to get as close as she could. Rex taught her to cook food that did not come straight out of a box, which was a skill that none of her friends had developed. She plucked pheasants, filleted trout, and baked scones and rock cakes in an Aga. There was something calming about the Highlands, and as the weeks went by, Karen's bump grew steadily, and her heart started to heal.

Karen still thought about Ernie every day. She could not forget that a huge part of her world had disappeared, and it happened to be the part she loved the most. From time to time she found herself alone, with nothing to do, and it was then she missed him most. Karen would have done anything to feel Ernie close to her once more, and for their lives to go back to how they had been. However, that was not the way it was. Life's croupier did not seem to care about her pain, and Ernie did not seem to care about anything.

"Stupid bastard!" thought her head, but her heart still loved him deeply.

o o o

It was a glorious, still autumn day. A translucent coat of frost covered the trees, and a lone cock pheasant called in the distance. The sea fog, or haar as it was known in those parts, drifted over the soft hills as if Avalon had returned to grace the world with her quiet presence. Karen was hoovering her room. Usually the mechanical movements of her arm and the humming of the vacuum cleaner put her in a state resembling meditation. Today was different. Her heart was heavy with thoughts of Ernie. Rex was downstairs, standing over an old steel mixing bowl in the kitchen. Up to his elbows in dumpling mix, he kneaded the thick dough with slow, deliberate movements as his mind drifted to a place of no thought. He enjoyed this place very much.

Karen had changed a great deal in the few weeks she had lived with Rex. His calmness had made her calmer and his optimism had rubbed off on her too. She had lost a lot but had gained something quite unique. However, today, her world was gloomy.

"Karen! Karen, my dear, come and look at my dumplings. I think you'll approve. We're going to have these sumptuous specimens with lamb and red wine gravy," Rex announced cheerfully, but his words were met with silence. "Karen? Karen? It's not good to stay in your room all day."

Nothing.

Rex cleaned the dough from his hands, washed them and placing a lid over the steel mixing bowl. As steady as ever, he walked up the creaking staircase to Karen's bedroom. It seemed to take an age for him to reach the top, his old joints creaking with every step. As he stood outside her room, he took a moment to compose himself, sensing what was going on inside. He knocked on the door. "Karen, dear," he asked gently, "can I come in?"

No reply.

Rex knocked on the door again. Still no reply. Opening it he found Karen curled up on her bed weeping.

"Oh, Karen, my dear. It's Ernie isn't it?" he asked, sitting down on the chair next to Karen's bed.

"I still love him, and it hurts. I hate it Rex. It's been three months and nothing. No letter, no phone call, no sign of Ernie at all. I spoke with Aunt Rose last night and he hasn't been in touch with her either. I have no idea where he is. How am I going to bring up a baby without a dad?" Karen wept, "I can't."

"Oh, my dear girl," Rex's deep voice replied, "you don't have to do this on your own. I'm not the baby's father, but I'm with you all the way and I'm not going anywhere. You're just having a bad day, that's all."

Karen turned to look at her new friend, tears smudged across her cheeks.

"Do you really think I'll be okay?"

"Yes, I do Karen. Things have a funny way of working out. We'll get through this, of course we will, and Rose wants to help too. That's a pretty strong team if you ask me," Rex told her, taking Karen's outstretched hand and holding it tightly.

"Ernie, Ernie, Ernie!" Karen sobbed into her pillow, her pregnant body shivering although it was not cold. "Stupid bastard!" she screamed. It was all so confusing. She looked at Rex through tear filled eyes and asked. "Why is this happening to me, Rex?"

But before Rex could reply, a deep inner knowing revealed itself to her. "No. It doesn't matter why this is happened. It's happening, and I have to get used to it. He's not coming back. I'm pretty sure he's not coming back," she said with a certain resignation. This time her sobbing was calmer, as if she was coming to terms with something she had been fighting for months. Rex sat on the chair holding her hand, silently. He was there for her and she knew that. There was nothing else he could do.

For two days Karen did not say a word. Her Romeo was gone. She would never again feel his touch, make love to him, or giggle as he laughed at one of his awful jokes. He was gone.

"Will anyone ever love me that much again?" she wondered, trying to imagine Ernie's warm body lying next to her, snoring softly. What was harder than remembering Ernie, was accepting that she was starting to forget him. At first it was the small details. It was not so easy to remember his smell, or the way he looked at her. His expressions became a blur in her mind's eye, and she hardly knew how it felt to be hugged by him. Ernie had abandoned her once, which was painful enough, and now he was dying in her mind.

Giving up on Ernie felt like a betrayal, but it also brought Karen a sense of peace. That peace told her she was making the right choice. She could not fight reality for the rest of her life, hoping that Ernie would return. That hope was ripping her apart. Looking at a tapestry hanging on the wall by her bed she gasped. She had not even seen it before, yet it depicted two angels staring into the sky, full of bliss. Underneath them were two sentences, sewn into the fabric of the tapestry.

"If you truly love someone, set them free. If they come back, they're yours; if they don't, they never were."

A memory of an evening she and Ernie had shared together, when Ernie was still grieving the loss of his mother, popped into her head. He had been inconsolable at the time, and Karen had reassured him he would be okay, and that life would never give him more than he could handle. She remembered Ernie looking hard into her eyes and saying,

"You're right Kazza, ah can handle this. Ah can deal with whatever life throws at me."

Karen had been surprised by what she had said. She had opened her mouth because it seemed like the right thing to do, but she was not even sure if it was true. Now, almost six months on, Karen was the one who was inconsolable, and it was her who was hoping her words had been the truth, and that *she* would get through this. She hoped that wherever Ernie was he was okay. He had taught her so much about love and laughter, and she would keep those precious months with him in her heart. She had been surrounded by violence from before she could remember and had not let it twist her into a resentful, acidic version of herself. At times she did want to hate Ernie, but she would not let hatred win. Only life's losers let hatred win.

"A brave person chooses to forgive," she whispered to herself, and if Karen was anything, she was brave. "I will never hate him. Never," she vowed, already feeling the worst was over.

o o o

Unbeknownst to Karen, a couple of hundred miles south, in a young offenders' institute tucked away in the moorlands of Northumbria her lost love was suffering too. The days dragged as Ernie rotated from toilet cleaning, to kitchen scrubbing, to whitewashing already white walls, doing his time and keeping his nose clean. The guards disliked him, the other prisoners were indifferent, and Karen did not reply to any of his letters, visit or answer his calls. Every Monday a trusted inmate would push a metal trolley with squeaky wheels around the cells, delivering post to those convicts fortunate enough to have someone on the outside who cared. Ernie lived for Mondays, hoping to get a letter, but the letter never came.

"She's given up on me."
"Why would she want a loser like me anyway?"

Although Ernie put a brave face on it, her silence ate him up. He spent his days thinking terrible thoughts about himself. He was helpless, like a fish caught in a trawler's net waiting to be hauled in and suffocated to death in the cold, salty air. A barbed wire noose was wrapped around Ernie's heart and slowly being pulled tight, and there was no way he could escape his fate. *"When will she send me a letter, like?"* he asked himself fifty times a day, but deep down he suspected the worst. The thoughts of self-loathing that had plagued much of his life now strangled his spirit.

Waiting in line at the breakfast queue with a thin metal tray clasped in both hands, Ernie fingered the tray and remembered the first time he had laid eyes on Karen. She had been standing in the dinner queue at school and had smacked an older boy over the head with a similar tray. As he allowed himself a hint of a smile, one of the guards sensed his moment of joy and went for him.

"Manning you ugly little scrote," the guard snarled, "stand up straight when you're in line, or you won't get anything." Then the guard put his face an inch from Ernie's and added. "Maggots like you deserve to rot in here." His breath smelled of hatred. The guard's cruel words stung, and the rest of Ernie's day was lost in a fog of anger and despondency.

That evening, lying on his hard, unforgiving mattress, watching a spider truss up a fly up in its steel chorded web, Ernie felt worse than he had done in many months. He could swallow his pride and clean toilets. He could bow his head and agree with the sadistic guards, and loneliness was nothing new to him, but those voices in his head, they just never let up. They followed him wherever he went.

"Ah killed me mam, and instead of trying to make something good of my life, ah became a

shoplifter and stole cars," they said. *"Then ah ruined everything with Kazza. Ah couldn't even be happy when she told me ah was ganna be a dad, like. Ah'm a scumbag, that's what ah am."* The guilt which hobbled after him felt like a delirious ghoul and he would have done anything to be finished with it. That night, as Ernie stared at the spider on the ceiling, his suffering had finally become too much to bear.

Bang.

Out of nowhere, Ernie's whole perception changed, and he knew he had come to a fork in the road of life. The road he had been walking was a road of suffering, and he had been walking it for long enough. The other road, the new one that had just revealed itself, was a mystery. It was a mystery because he had never walked it before. It was a road where he stopped listening to the voices in his head and chose to let go of their negativity.

"Ah'm not ganna think about all this shit anymore. It does me head in," he told himself. "Ah'm not ganna let the guards break me either. Ah'm ganna do me time, get out, find Karen and make things right." He suddenly felt older than his years, as if he had paid an old debt with pain, and the debt was now cleared. He had been best friends with adversity all his life, and it was yet to kill him. "Ah'm ganna be strong," he vowed. "Ah'm ganna walk out of prison with me head held high." Nobody knew it, but the shy, retiring Geordie was at his best when his back was against the wall. "Ah'm ganna get out of this rat pit in one piece, find Karen and win her back. If it's the last thing ah do."

o o o

It was the summer of 1961. The year that Carl Jung passed away at the ripe old age of 85 and Boy George was born in Bexley Heath. The holidays had arrived, and Virginia was in seventh heaven. Hurray! The intrepid nine-year-old had no more school for nearly three months. It was glorious, at last she could relax and play, and have adventures away from those hard-boiled teachers who did not know the meaning of the word "fun".

Virginia finished her cornflakes, hugged her mother, grabbed her older brother by the hand, and raced down to the Willow Grove at the bottom of the garden giggling to herself. Her home in Hampshire was special and she knew it. Toads burped, songbirds sang, and the little girl spent the afternoons fishing for minnows in the river that meandered through the Grove. There were seven huge willow trees on its banks, their drooping branches perfect for climbing and swinging. She and her brother and sister would play hide and seek in the rushes or wade into the mud looking for duck nests and otters. Virginia loved to pull herself up into the branches of her favourite tree, hugging its trunk and watching, pretending to be a hawk; watching, waiting, quiet and alert. It was delightful to be aware of the sounds and the smells and experience the joy of life happening by itself. It did not take more than a few minutes for the animals to show themselves once they thought they were alone, and often a water vole or an otter would swim by. It was going to be the best summer of Virginia's short life and she did not have a care in the world.

o o o

It was a Tuesday and Virginia's siblings were going into Winchester for the day with their mother.

"Susan just called. She'll be here in ten minutes. We have to go, or we'll miss Peter's appointment. Will you be okay on your own for ten minutes?" her mother asked.

"I'll be fine. Susan's always late," Virginia replied.

"Okay Vig. Be good, and don't go to the Grove unless you're with Susan. I love you." He mother kissed her daughter on the forehead and the three of them left.

Virginia's life did not have too many rules, but if she ever went to the Grove alone, she would be in big trouble. She waited a whole half of an hour, and still no sign of Susan the babysitter.

"Where are you Susan? Come on, I want to go out and play." Looking out of the kitchen window Virginia could see the sun shining, and the distant ripples of the river dancing in the light. "Maybe if I stay away from the river?" Virginia thought rebelliously, and finally she could not resist it anymore. Wearing a simple, old-fashioned, white cotton frock that her mother had made her, Virginia wandered down to the Willow Grove alone to see what she could find. She climbed a tree, skimmed some pebbles, got her dress covered in grass stains, and then lay back on the soft lawn and looked up at the sky. As a warm blade of grass tickled her neck and the smell of summer filled her nose, a horde of swallows darted overhead, cutting their wings through the air with an elegance that was absent from the human world. Virginia stared at them, transfixed.

Suddenly her trance was broken by an unfamiliar noise. It sounded like a mouse scurrying around in the undergrowth, but it was not a mouse, it was bigger. The young girl in the old-fashioned dress sprang to her feet and trotted towards the noise.

"Squeak."

Whatever it was, it was on the other side of the river, and it moved like lightning. Virginia kicked off her sandals, and without thinking of taking off her dress or the fact that she was about to break the gravest of rules, she jumped into the river and swam to the far shore. It was fun to pretend to be a cat stalking its prey, and more fun because she had no idea what her prey was. Directing her ears into the undergrowth she could hear nothing save the faint whisper of the wind in the reeds. The sound was gone.

"Squeak, squeak."

There it was again, probably no more than five yards ahead of her.

"I'm not going to lose you this time," she thought, and ran towards the noise as fast as her legs would carry her. In a flash Virginia found herself only a few feet away from a strange brown rodent, which held her gaze for a second and then shot into some bushes to her left. Virginia gave chase once more, pushing the branches aside and skipping through, keeping the creature in sight. It was fast. The small, brown animal disappearing into a hedge at the edge of the field as quickly as it had arrived, and Virginia followed, half

climbing, half diving through the brambly shrubs, ignoring the scratches on her arms. Suddenly, the darkness of the shrubs was replaced by sunlight and she found herself stumbling onto a tarmac road.

There was no way Virginia could avoid the speeding sports car. As the driver slammed on the brakes, the nine-year-old was mesmerised by the hunk of metal bearing down on her, frozen to the spot. At the last instant she closed her eyes and instinctively held her breath. The brakes squealed, the tyres screeched, and the driver turned sharply to avoid the soaking wet girl in the white dress.

Virginia opened her eyes just in time to see the sturdy trunk of a two hundred-year-old oak tree take the full impact of the car. The driver, who was a large, bald man, was thrown forward, violently head-butting the windscreen and smashing it to pieces. The wrench of twisted metal, and the whip of the driver's head as it thudded into the windscreen, would be etched into her memory for years. It was no sight for a little girl to see.

Then everything went quiet.

Virginia stood stock-still.

"This is my fault. I am going to be in so much trouble," she panicked. "Mummy told me never to go to the grove alone. Oh no." Ghostly white, Virginia watched smoke billowing from the bonnet of the car, and could see that the bodywork was folded over itself

like tinfoil. The enormous driver was hunched over the steering wheel, unmoving. "Please, don't be dead," she prayed, her eyes scrunched together, and her fingers crossed. A thick shard of glass was sticking out of his shoulder, blood oozing from the gash. Virginia bit her lip to stop herself crying. "What have I done? What have I done? Oh, Mummy, Mummy help me!" Then she heard the sound of another car approaching, and without waiting to see who it was, Virginia ran back across the road and dived into the shrubbery. From the safety of her hiding place she watched the driver stop his car and rush out to help the bald man. Then she turned away and ran all the way home without looking back.

CHAPTER 10

Russian Roulette

It was the summer of 1987. Prozac hit the market for the first time and Aretha Franklin finally got the respect she deserved. Twenty-seven winters had come and gone since the nine-year-old Virginia had vowed never to go to the Willow Grove alone again. That day had been tucked away in her subconscious and was not something she dwelled on much at all. Life goes on, everyone makes mistakes, and now she was a Geography teacher with a husband she loved and a happy life.

This sixth form field trip to East Shields was her fourth this year and the part of teaching she enjoyed the most. It was a long journey from the Midlands, but time had flown by, as the coach was filled with laughter. There were twenty sixth-form students and two other teachers in the bus. Chester Bradfield, a South African exchange teacher, and Reginald Taylor, the Head of Geography, who was considered a legend in his own lifetime. Reginald, like many of his kind, was stocky, down to earth, and had a thick working-class accent. As Head of Geography it was his task to give the students their assignment for the day, and he grabbed this opportunity with both hands.

"Your task," he began, spitting out the work 'task' like a machine gun bullet, "is to explore the docklands with a fine, tooth comb. Take notes on the different types of land use and interview any locals who can't run away quick enough. Whatever you do be nice to them, we want to be able to come back some day," he smiled. "Oh, yes, and meet back at the bus at five o'clock sharp. I'd like to say we won't wait for you if you're late," he smiled again, "but of course, we're not going leave you stranded in this Hinterland. It wouldn't go down too well with your parents or the Child Protection Agency, and God knows what might happen to you this far North. So, please be on time and we can stop for fish and chips on the way home." The meaning underneath Reginald's words was that the students should disappear, find a nice café, make up a few interviews with locals, and enjoy themselves without interference from the staff. *Vis a vis,* the teachers were required to disappear in another direction, find a nice café, and enjoy themselves without interference from the pupils. It was the perfect recipe for a happy day. The students cheered, and Virginia smiled. Reginald's sarcasm and good humour seemed to turn everything into an adventure.

Once they were out of sight of the students, Chester took out a cigarette and waved it in front of Virginia's nose.

"Come on Vig, you gotta try it, just to see what it's like."

"You only want me to smoke because you can't catch me on the hockey pitch," Virginia replied sarcastically. However, there was something about being pressured into having a cigarette by a fellow teacher that appealed to her. Virginia had gone through thirteen years of school and three years of college without ever touching a cigarette. Her friends had teased her, cajoled her and tried to trick her into smoking, but she had held out. Why? Because she knew how unhealthy it was, but could one cigarette be all that bad?

"Alright Chester," she gave in, "I'll try, but only to shut you up."

"Good girl," said Chester, "Try one of these. I confiscated a pack of them yesterday. It's very light," he winked as he handed a cigarette to Virginia. She stopped walking, took the cigarette and pursed it between her lips. Chester lit it with his Guns n' Roses Zippo lighter, and Virginia started to laugh.

"That is so cheesy Chester. Guns and Roses? Come on."

"Not my fault. I confiscated this too. Now focus on the cigarette Vig. No distractions," replied Chester with a wry grin. Taking her first drag, a look of surprise came over Virginia's face.

"It's not that bad," she exclaimed, surprised.

"Well done," Reginald pipped in, enjoying the opportunity to witness a fellow teacher corrupt another fellow teacher, and Virginia smiled.

"I could get used to this smoking business."

Both Chester and Reginald lit up, and the three school teachers chatted away about nothing.

An hour later Virginia, Chester and Reginald were wandering through housing estates, talking and laughing together, celebrating the fact that they were being paid to do something they would willingly do for free.

"Looks pretty dark up there," said Reginald, staring at the blackening sky. Before his words had come, out the rain streamed down as only northern rain can. Heavy, hard and without mercy, it bounced off puddles so aggressively it felt that it was raining from below, spitting upwards from the earth itself. The three amigos sprinted to the shelter of a nearbye bus stop.

"This calls for something a little stronger," said Chester as he lit up a Marlboro Red.

"Can I have one of those?" Virginia asked.

"I'm not sure that's such a good idea, Vig. These are different, they're much stronger," Chester replied.

"Well. I'm not going to get addicted on my first day, am I?"

"Okay lassie, if that's what you want."

As the teachers sheltered in an ordinary looking bus stop, outside an ordinary looking house, in an ordinary part of East Shields, Virginia took her first drag on an ordinary looking Marlboro cigarette.

"Holy shit," she gasped as her lungs burned and her eyes watered.

"Very lady like, Vig," laughed Chester, as Virginia embarked on a thirty second coughing fit.

"I don't think Phillip Morris has found a new life long customer," chuckled Reginald, putting a comforting hand on Virginia's back. Virginia looked at the cigarette as if it had just punched her in the face.

"You can't inhale that deeply the first time, you mug," Chester laughed, but for Virginia there was not going to be a second time. She glared at the cigarette in her hand one last time and then tossed it over the wall behind her.

"Screw that Chester. You're the mug putting

that crap into your body," she countered between coughs.

"Come on, let's get back to the bus," suggested Reginald. So, the three of them pulled up their hoods and walked back to the coach in the rain.

Unknown to Virginia, her second ever cigarette had flown through the air, still alight, and landed in a pile of newspapers stacked by the front door of number twelve Acacia Avenue. Ten minutes later, the ground floor was ablaze, and the flames licking their way upwards. Aunt Rose was in her bedroom hoovering and had no idea that in minutes the smoke would knock her out and the searing heat of the flames would kill her. She never felt a thing as the fire engulfed the whole house, destroying everything inside it, including her.

o o o

Ernie was frog marched through the labyrinth of damp corridors that made it all but impossible to leave the prison unless the authorities deemed it fit. His cold fingers were tightly curled around his crutches and a guard's heavy hand pressed down on his shoulder, making it more difficult for him to hobble. However, he was hobbling towards the exit gates, and no matter what tricks the guard might play on him, Ernie knew that very soon he would be free. He hardly noticed the smell of rusted metal or the graffitied walls that cloaked the prison in despair. The smell of steel had shocked him when he had first arrived, but he had soon become accustomed to it and then forgot it was even a smell at all. There was no other place Ernie had ever been, nor expected to go, where metal had its own stench which induced its own torrid emotion.

Ernie was released the day before his birthday in 1987, a month early for good behaviour. It was a profoundly altered man who left the claustrophobic confines of the young offenders' institute. The teenaged Geordie had survived borstal, but five months had felt like a decade, and his face carried this hardship for all to see. His eyes, which had radiated a certain childlike innocence, were harder and more distant, as if a great weight had fallen on his slim shoulders pinning him to the floor. His body was gaunt, but passing the time doing press ups in his cell, had imbued his sinuous arms with deceptive strength.

6.00 a.m. The heavy iron gates parted with a jarring clang. Ernie crossed his fingers and prayed his Juliet would be on the other side waiting for him. Perhaps she wanted him back? Perhaps Karen would be there, beaming at him with that knowing smile, the way she used to when they were together. It might take time, but they could work things out.

"Stay out of trouble Manning you little scrote, and make sure we never see you again," spat the guard. The grinding of an oversized key in a cumbersome lock was the last sound Ernie heard before he was ejected from Her Majesty's pleasure. He was tempted to give the guard the finger but held himself back.

"Ah'm not giving you the satisfaction," he muttered through gritted teeth. Ernie was wearing the same red Nike tracksuit he had been arrested in, and apart from his clothes the only possessions he had were a plastic bag containing his Mickey Mouse watch, a prison issue toothbrush and one pound fifty for the bus.

"Those heartless pricks didn't even give us breakfast, like," he thought sullenly, then scanned the car park for any sign of Karen. There were a couple of white prison vans, a dodgy looking Ford Capri, and a bored kitchen worker grabbing a smoke before strolling back into the canteen, but no Karen. Ernie's heart sank, but he was not going to give up. It was early, and if he waited a while she might turn up. He brushed the dirt off a concrete step, laid his crutches by his side, and sat down by the forbidding prison gates waiting for Karen to arrive.

7.00 a.m. The dodgy looking Capri was driven

away by a guard with long, greasy hair coming off the night shift, no doubt eager to get home to the comfort of his bed. A third white prison van joined the others, but still no Karen. Ernie's optimism started to wane. *"She's not coming,"* he thought, beginning to face what was becoming a lonely inevitability.

7.30 a.m. A car appeared in the distance. The rising sun shone into Ernie's eyes, stopping him from seeing the driver clearly, but it looked like a woman. His heart missed a beat. The Capri skidded to a halt, and the greasy haired guard who had left half an hour before, rushed past security to fetch something he had forgotten. Ernie could have asked him for a lift but his face was cruel and Ernie thought the better of it.

9.00 a.m. *"Who am ah kidding, like? She's not coming."* Karen had had the good sense to move on with her life and Ernie was not a part of it.

10.00 a.m. Ernie was bored, and his bum was aching. Stretching like an old alley cat, he set his gaze on the prison car park exit.

"Number twelve Acacia Avenue," he whispered to himself. Karen and Aunt Rose's home was thirteen miles away, and on crutches it could take him days to get there, but it was the only place he could think of going. It was closer than his own home, and if Karen was there it would be worth the walk. "No time like the present," he muttered, and without looking back at the pain he had left behind, he started to hobble towards the main road hoping for a lift. Surely someone would pick up a cripple hitch hiking in the middle of nowhere on the A68?

5.00 p.m. A few cars had passed but no-one had stopped. Forcing himself to keep going, the familiar thoughts that had plagued Ernie for months churned around his head, all of them offering nothing but suffering.

"She doesn't want me."
"She's met someone else."
"Someone a lot better than me."

Half a dozen cars passed him, but none stopped to pick up the scruffy youth with the plastic bag.

7.00 p.m. Ernie's feet were blistered and raw, and his armpits squealed in pain with every step, but he kept going.

"At least it's not raining," he thought.

He could not resist stealing a bunch of tulips from a petrol station forecourt. The flowers were not the best, but they had to make do, as there were no graveyards nearby. Seconds later, as if the Gods were punishing him for his crime, a crash of thunder shook the ground beneath him, and a heavy downpour descended from the clouds above. Within minutes Ernie was shivering, soaked through by freezing rain. It was now even harder going, and the wet aggravated his blisters, transforming his feet into balls of fire.

10.30 p.m. Too many layers of pedal skin later. A bright blue Robin Reliant pulled up beside the disheveled young man. He was still six miles from East Shields, the sun had set two hours before, and hypothermia was on the cards.

"You look awfully cold. Do you need a lift?" asked a kindly voice from behind the wheel. "I'm heading to East Shields."

"You're a life saver," Ernie replied. "Ah'd love a lift to East Shields." Ernie bundled himself into the tiny, three-wheeler, and half an hour later the kindly woman dropped him off at the bus stop outside Karen's home. It was dark, and he was exhausted, but the flutter of nervousness in his stomach filled him with renewed energy.

"Thank you, ah owe you one," he told her, and she smiled back sympathetically.

"Good luck. I hope you get her back," came her reply, then the Reliant spluttered away. Tucking the flowers behind his back, Ernie composed himself, and then walked into Karen's driveway.

There were no lights on, and Aunt Rose's car was not in the driveway.

"That's strange," Ernie thought, as he peered into the blackness of the night. Looking closer at the silhouette of the old house he knew so well, he gasped. "The roof's gone! Oh shit, the roof's not there." Hobbling closer to the building a sight he never imagined he would ever see became starkly obvious. The walls of Karen's home were charred black, and the windows shattered. The roof had burned to a crisp and collapsed into the house. "Oh my God," he gasped again. Then Ernie limped around the back of the house as fast as he could.

Peering into Karen's bedroom, the sight that met Ernie's exhausted eyes was beyond the worst of his nightmares. Her room was no more than an empty shell. The floor had collapsed, leaving a mass of charred floorboards lying in a blackened heap. The wallpaper too was scorched black, and all that was left of Karen's bed were melted, metal springs protruding from the ashes. Nothing had survived. No pictures, no furniture, no Aunt Rose, no Karen. He lent against the wall of number twelve Acacia Avenue. All the strength having left his legs and he slid down the cold, stone wall collapsing at the bottom in a heap. Lying on the sharp pebbles outside Karen's home, unable to move, unable to breath, Ernie broke down and began to wail.

o o o

Standing outside the police station, staring at the dark blue sign hanging above the entrance, Ernie felt afraid. In prison he had learned to distrust the authorities, and nothing had happened since his release to suggest he was wrong about that. However, needing to know what had happened to Karen and her aunt made walking through his fear and the police station doors a necessity. Had they survived?

"There was a fire at number twelve Acacia Avenue, and ah wanted to find out what happened to the two ladies who lived there," Ernie asked the policeman in reception. The policeman, who was skimming through a notepad at the time, looked up and slowly walked over to Ernie.

"And who might you be?" he asked, looking him up and down.

"Erm. Well. Ah, erm." The clang of prison locks and the stench of rusted iron returned, and even though Ernie had nothing to hide he wouldn't give the policeman anything. "It doesn't matter," Ernie muttered, turned around and left.

o o o

"What was ah thinking, like?" Ernie thought to himself. *"The police weren't going to tell me anything. Ah'm nobody. Even if ah told them me name, it wouldn't make any difference. It's not written anywhere that ah've ever had anything to do with her. Ah can't prove ah was Karen's boyfriend or that her baby is mine."* He paused, for the first time reflecting on the fact that his unborn child might also have perished in the blaze. He shrugged that painful thought off. *"Ah need a plan,"* he thought instead.

"Hello, me name's Barry, erm Johnson, ah wondered if ah could take a look at some papers in your archives? Ah'm particularly interested in the Acacia Avenue fire."

"Certainly. I think that was last Tuesday's edition, right? " replied the young journalist who answered the phone.

"Yes, that's it," replied Ernie. *"Oh my God, it was only a week ago. If only ah'd been out, ah could've done something."*

"Come over any time before four."

The story was all over the front page, with a large photo of a house covered in flames. Karen´s house. Without taking take time sit down, Ernie read:

"The Fire Brigade were called to a blaze at a home in Acacia Avenue, East Shields at 3.00 a.m. on Tuesday.

Ian Black, area commander for Northumbria Fire and Rescue Service, says crews arrived to find "the home engulfed by the blaze" with "smoke and flames coming out of the ground floor and upstairs windows." He says firemen eventually managed to enter the house to try to rescue those inside, but at least one person had died. Rose Smith, originally from Hunstanton, had suffocated, and her niece, Karen Walsh, was still unaccounted for.

"Rose Smith was well loved, and the local community is in a state of shock at this time. If anyone has any information about the possible whereabouts of Miss Walsh, please come forward."

Mr. Black says officers will work with Northumbrian Police to establish the cause of the blaze, but at present it is not being treated as suspicious."

Still standing up, Ernie read the article again.

"Oh God, she might be alive. She must be alive! I have to find her." His heart pounded as if it was trying to escape from his chest. The trail was still fresh. If Karen was alive he could find her.

Ernie remembered something his mother had done years before that he could try now. He closed his eyes and focused on tuning into Karen. He thought Karen's name to himself and waited to see what would happen in the space after that thought. Nothing. Quiet, silent, awareness, but no answer. Then...

Out of the void two simple words emerged in his head.

"Rose's funeral." Of course! If Karen was alive, she would go to her Aunt's funeral.

Ernie went to the table where today´s edition of the East Shields Gazette was displayed. He quickly thumbed to the Births and Deaths section. Sure enough, there it was! Rose Smith's funeral was at two o'clock in the afternoon on Monday the 13th at Little Shields Chapel.

"What day is it today?" Ernie asked the woman behind the counter.

"It's Monday," she replied, stifling a yawn.

"Oh shit, what time is it?"

"Quarter past two."

Ernie dropped the paper, stumbled down the stairs and hobbled towards Little Shields Church as fast as he could.

o o o

There were less than a dozen people at the funeral, most of them women over seventy years old. Karen sat a few pews away from the other mourners, sobbing into a handkerchief and hoping not to be noticed. She didn´t know any of them, and she had no desire to get to know them and have to explain her big belly that was impossible to cover up anymore. It was a short service, just over half an hour, and as the organ started playing the final hymn, Karen quietly headed for the double doors. A tall man in a long coat approached her.

"I'm sorry to disturb you Maam but are you Karen Walsh?" he asked.

"Yes, that's me," Karen replied.

"Thank God you're alive."

With ringing in his ears, Ernie crashed through the church doors. Utter silence. No one was there. No funeral, only a trainee priest setting up candles for a service later that week.

"Is this Little Shields Chapel?" Ernie panted.

"Nope. This is the church. Little Shields Chapel is the other side of town, near Cathy's tea shop."

"No!" shouted Ernie, throwing his crutches down on the hard, stone floor. The crash echoed through the church. The trainee gave him a startled look and opened his mouth to say something. Before he got the chance, Ernie had picked up his crutches and left.

By luck he was able to hail a taxi back at the

main road, and he arrived at the Chapel at a quarter past three. A group of old women were standing in the entrance, talking about the weather.

"Excuse me. Has there just been a funeral here?"

"Yes, love."

"Was there a pretty, eighteen-year old girl with brown hair here?"

All of the women looked at one another. They had not noticed Karen sitting towards the back.

"No, just us and a tall man in a long coat. No youngsters I'm afraid. They never seem to want to come to these things."

o o o

It may have seemed doomed, but Ernie was not ready to give up on the small glimmer of hope that Karen was alive. For the following weeks he visited all the places Karen used to hang out and asked anyone he could about her. Carrying the photograph of the two of them in his jacket, the one from that glorious day in Seahouses, he asked and asked and asked, but no-one had seen her.

Often when he took the picture out, people would complement him on having such a beautiful girlfriend, but nothing came of their complements.

"Yeh, she used to come here most afternoons, but I haven't seen her in a few weeks," he was told time and again.

No-one had any idea where Karen Walsh had gone, but wherever she was, she obviously did not want Ernie to find her. Or maybe she *had* died in that fire? Then Ernie got the idea that she might have returned to Huntstapleton. He sold most of his mother's furniture in a hurry and bought a train ticket south. In Huntstapleton he found no trace of her either, and after a couple of weeks he gave up and returned home to nothing.

"*The good times never last.*"

o o o

Once he was discharged from hospital, Kevin's life continued much as it had before he was assaulted by the man he had tried to help. He had nightmares from time to time, and unexpected eruptions of rage, but once his injuries had healed, Kevin thought he had put the whole episode behind him. However, what no-one at the hospital had discovered, was that Kevin had a tiny blood clot hiding deep inside his brain caused by the severity of the beating. This blood clot was growing a little bigger every day which meant that Kevin, who was to all intents and purposes the most ordinary of people, was a time bomb waiting to explode. It was merely a question of when.

One sunny Saturday afternoon Kevin and Brenda's next door neighbours took a day trip to Whipsnell Safari Park. The monkeys made them laugh, the polar bears looked hot and bothered, and the chimpanzees were having the time of their life. However, as Kevin's neighbours drove into the Savannah Adventure area of the park, things took a turn for the worse.

Eye witnesses reported that Magnus, a male white rhino, had, in an innocent bid to find female companionship, taken a fancy to the Shogun. As the people carrier had driven into the enclosure, he had snorted flirtatiously and brushed his flanks against the side of the vehicle, letting out a deep, carnal bellow as he did. The shortsighted beast could feel the hard metal against his thighs and the softer, more malleable rubber of the tyres against his snout. He soon got himself worked up into a frenzy. Magnus was not the rhino world's most enthusiastic advocate for foreplay, so without wasting any time he climbed on top of the Shogun to give it the good news. A few amorous thrusts later, Magnus had made short work of the vehicle, crushing the cab, buckling the doors and tearing the roof clean off. In a bid to escape the attention of the randy beast, the terrified family leapt from the close to exploding wreck. However, unfortunately for them, they failed to spot a hungry lioness and her cubs lurking close by. None of them lived to tell the tale.

Amongst optimists, it is commonly believed that every cloud has a silver lining, and in this case it probably did. The neighbour's next of kin took pity on Magnus, and rather than selling the battered Shogun for scrap, they donated it to the zoo. To this day, if on a quiet evening one happens to wander by Whipsnell Safari Park, one can still sometimes hear the dull thud of rhino flesh against crushed metal, as Magnus furnishes his unresponsive, but seemingly willing bride with a bit of loving.

o o o

For weeks Ernie did not smile, he did not laugh, and the simple tasks like brushing his teeth felt like climbing Mount Everest at night in a blizzard. Waking up, he would glimpse perhaps a minute of calm, before the hellish thoughts returned, like a sea of misery sweeping through him. These thoughts meant only one thing, yet another day of anguish lay ahead of him, before he could finally collapse into the blessed relief of sleep. The mornings were the hardest. Not a glimmer of hope or enjoyment, not a hint that any part of life was worth living. Getting out of bed in the morning was like crawling through quicksand, and it was an achievement that he managed to feed himself even the tiniest morsel of food. In the darkest days of despair and dread he did not achieve even that. He stayed in bed, slowly starving and praying for the mercy that death would bring. The good days were murder, but at least he managed to prop himself up on his mother's old sofa and watch television for a few hours. Filling himself with bad news and crappy daytime TV programmes partially distracted him from the agony of being alive.

The bad days? Well, it was a miracle that his heart kept beating. On those days, and they came all too often, the darkness of his mind consumed every part of his being. Fear, paranoia, shame, disgust, guilt, they called it clinical depression. If he would have had the energy to give it a name Ernie would have called it living death. He had lost his mother and his true love, and spent the best part of a year in prison being ignored and abused. He could not cope with planet earth anymore. It was time to leave.

o o o

Later that year a new family replaced the tragic, safari loving family who had lived next to Kevin and Brenda. The Jacksons were not the typical middle-class village type that the village were hoping for. They hailed from Grimsby and were as working class as battered haddock and chips, swilled down with a diet coke and ending with an enormous burb. Mrs. Jackson had won a six-figure settlement, thanks to an unscrupulous no-win no-fee lawyer, a great deal of good luck, and the over-enthusiastic health and safety laws that were sweeping the country at the time. The Jacksons were anything but quiet, anonymous or reserved, and stuck out like a sore thumb. They announced their arrival by erecting a gigantic, pink letterbox at the end of their driveway. Amongst the subtle greys and conservative blues of the other post boxes, it caused quite a stir, and brought disapproving comments and tuts from the other residents. They tutted fervently from behind net curtains, but none of them had the courage to say anything about it in person. Rather they hoped it would be the last of such social transgressions. However, the post box was merely a prelude for the impending nightmare the Jacksons were going to unleash on the neighbourhood. David Jackson, a beer bellied, homemade tattooed, shaven-headed thug, owned a rather unpleasant Alsatian called Killer.

"Kiiiiillllllleeeerrrr. Bloody 'ell. Don't crap in their garden, Killer," he would scream at the top of his lungs whilst walking back from the pub at eleven o'clock at

night. "Faaaking 'ell Killer, putt that faaking poodle down."

The neighbour's curtains would twitch and their blood pressure spike, but still none dared speak to him. He was far working class to engage in conversation, particularly if that conversation risked offending him. When Mr. Jackson was not fighting or throwing up in the women's toilet at the pub, he spent his time in an armchair in his living room, a beer in hand and a cigarette hanging from his meaty fingers. To make matters worse, the Jacksons blasted out heavy metal music until the wee hours, and attracted all the wrong types of people; punks, cons, ex-cons, motorcycle gangs, and on one occasion a van of riot police. Kevin and Brenda's peace and quiet was shattered beyond recognition. Kevin hardly slept for weeks.

Finally, after the Jacksons' third all-nighter in a row, he mustered up the courage to ask them to keep it down. Wandering over to their front door, Kevin wondered if it really was worth the hassle. Mr. Jackson looked like the kind of person you did not want to make an enemy of.

"Just be polite Kevin. No need to be abrasive," he reassured himself, and before he knew it, he was ringing the doorbell. Thunder by ACDC replaced the normal chimes, and a minute later Mr. Jackson's imposing frame appeared at the door.

"I'm sorry to disturb you," Kevin apologized nervously, as he stood on Mr. Jackson's doorstep feeling far too exposed for comfort. At first Mr. Jackson ignored the accountant, instead looking into the distance for Killer. Kevin cleared his throat. It was dry and he was not sure if he was even able to talk.

"Erm, Mr. Jackson. Erm, Kevin Stainforth, I erm live right over there." He pointed to his home. "I don't mean to interfere or be rude in any way, but my wife and I. Well, erm, we really wish you would keep the noise down. You've had so many parties since you moved in, and this is a quiet, residential area and…"

Mr. Jackson raised an eyebrow as he interrupted.

"Do you know how to spell broken nose?" he asked Kevin, a thuggish look of stupidity on his face.

"Erm, yes," Kevin replied cautiously. "I do have a degree."

"Well, I do to and if you don't piss off now, I'm going to show you."

Mr. Jackson's words made no sense, but the mention of a broken nose was enough to convince Kevin that it was best not to push this matter any further. He backed away, keeping his eyes to the ground and scurried home to Brenda.

Over the following months, Kevin's world was turned upside down, as Mr. Jackson and his family *tightened their grip on the village. Kevin no longer washed his car on Sundays, and he was terrified that he might bump into Mr. Jackson in the street. His mental declined dramatically. The blood clot in his brain was expanding and his bouts of rage worsening. Kevin could not sleep, and his relationship with Brenda deteriorated. Brenda did not like having the Jacksons next door, but she could not understand why the whole saga had changed Kevin so much. He was so different. So unreliable. So agitated. Brenda started to go into herself. She spent more and more time out of the house, writing her book in the library, and avoiding Kevin when she could. She started to fall out of love with the man she believed she would be with forever, and it hurt. Every time she mustered up the courage to talk to him, he seemed so far away, so unresponsive.*

After many months of living with a man she hardly knew anymore, Brenda called her mother, and then walked out on Kevin leaving only a note.

Kevin read the note at half past three in the afternoon.

3.31pm...

...splish.

Never again would Kevin run his fingers through

Brenda's bowl haircut, or sit next to her quietly in the living room as they worked on separate Sudoku puzzles. All he noticed was a bit of dizziness, but within seconds part of his brain was flooded and starved of oxygen. The old, amenable Kevin died, and someone sinister was born. Out of the flames of normality, in a tiny, irrelevant, middle-class village in the Home Counties, hidden under the sterile cloak of suburbia, emerged the Kevin the Terrorist.

CHAPTER 11

Dr. Fritz

Ernie sat cross-legged on his bed, a bottle of cheap Kurdish vodka and a bottle of sedatives lay on the duvet in front of him. He hoped it was enough to do the job, and he would soon be free of his misery. He unscrewed both bottle tops and turned to look at the photograph standing on his bedside table. The smiling image of he and Karen at Seahouses looked almost surreal, like it had happened in another life.

"Cheers, Kazza. Ah know it didn't work out, but ah'm really glad ah met you, like. Here's to the old times," he toasted, raising the vodka bottle in the air. With trembling hands Ernie then emptied the white pills into his mouth. Their bitter taste felt like acid burning his tongue, so he quickly guzzled two or three gulps of the hard liquor to swill them down. As soon as he had done this he began to cough violently, dribble mixed with vodka pouring from his mouth, staining the bedsheets with spittle and pills. He spat the rest of the pills out and frantically ran a finger around his mouth to make sure none remained. He could not stop coughing, and ironically, he began to fear that he might choke to death.

Exhausted, Ernie finally calmed down and his breathing returned to normal. He looked at two bottles, and then at the photograph again, feeling an enormous sense of stupidity and guilt. "What are you doing, man?" he groaned. "Foock. Ah need help."

o o o

An ambulance drove Ernie to an emergency psychiatric unit where he spent a few days being assessed. As had been the case when he was recovering from the ambulance incidence, Ernie enjoyed being looked after. It was a big relief to not have to struggle on alone, and his depression slowly started to lift.

o o o

Ernie made his way through the labyrinth of

hospital corridors, as he had done every week for the previous month. Eventually he found himself on the wrong side of the heavy oak doors to Dr. Fritz's office. Ernie hated those doors. They weighed more than he did and were hinged with industrial strength springs which almost beheaded him every time he tried to get through them. He somehow squeezed his way into the softly lit room, knowing how it felt to be mayonnaise squeezed from a tube. Nursing a bruised arm and feeling less than capable, he looked up to see the psychiatrist, as usual sitting behind his oversized mahogany desk.

"Ha! Nothing like a bit of a physical challenge to get you going in the morning," Dr. Fritz exclaimed enthusiastically. The doctor's words emerged from his most distinguished feature, a magnificent bushy beard which covered most of his upper torso. It was jet black, except for a stripe of pure white hair about an inch wide which ran down the middle of it. The beard exploded from his face like a wild animal, and yet behind it, no matter what happened, Dr. Fritz remained impressively calm. He was a small man with a face that belonged to a Greek philosopher. His large nose, prominent cheekbones and wavy black hair gave the impression of someone whose intelligence was matched only by his enhanced psychic perception. Dr. Eric Raphael Eustis Fritz MD's office was the only place in the hospital where the harsh strip lights had been removed and replaced with the gentle, warm glow of traditional lamps. The whole feeling of his room was safe, steady and intellectual, suitable for a man who had got it all together. Dr. Fritz motioned to a black leather chair in the centre of the room, into which Ernie then collapsed, letting his crutches clatter noisily to the floor.

"Oops, sorry, like."

The doctor dismissed Ernie's apology with a casual wave of his hand, whilst finishing scribbling his notes on a previous patient. The young Geordie's gaze meandered around the office, which happened to be one of his favourite places in the world. There was something regal about this place, something old and impressive. It was a time capsule, full of dusty bookshelves and drawings of racehorses and bare-chested boxers on the walls. Ernie noted that distinguished people made a habit of surrounding themselves with valuable wood.

"Ah'll never be able to do that," Ernie thought to himself. *"Ah'll never have enough money."* Ernie had only known Dr. Fritz for a month but trusted him implicitly. Here was someone who had compassion and understanding for Ernie's problems, a man who could relate to him on a level no-one else had done since Karen had been on the scene. Someone who was ready

to help and give Ernie the guidance he so desperately needed.

Dr. Fritz placed his bulbous, crimson fountainpen onto his desk and began to look at his patient thoughtfully. They both sat in silence, surrounded by dusty hardbacks, as Dr. Fritz's wise eyes surveyed Ernie and his clinical mind bore deep into his psyche.

"You seem to be quite tired, my boy. You struggled more than usual with my doors."

"There's only two buses a day between here and East Shields, like. Ah have to walk about a mile and a half just to get here. And your doors, and they just about kill me no matter how strong ah feel. What's with them?"

"Well, I'm not a sadist," Dr. Fritz replied, stroking his thumb and index finger through his beard. "They're a way of seeing how you're doing. How we face even small challenges changes dramatically with our mental state. The doors tell me a lot about my patients. But anyway, it's not good that you have to walk so far. I'll tell you what, I'll organize for a taxi or an ambulance to pick you up. We've got funds for that sort of thing."

"Thanks so much, Dr. Fritz. You're a class act," replied Ernie, momentarily breaking out of his melancholy. Ernie's mind began to wander, and he found himself wondering if Dr. Fritz's beard was the result of being attacked by a rabid skunk? Or perhaps he was halfway through eating a badger? Either way Ernie liked the beard, which added something indefinable to the corduroy clad genius.

"Yes," the doctor declared slowly, bringing Ernie out of his daydream, "definitely." Another pause, and then a quick fiddle with the badger's bottom, "your eyes look a little brighter. Indeed, yes, brighter than last week. I know it's not all sunshine and rainbows, but you are moving in the right direction."

"That's really good to hear," replied Ernie, feeling a wave of relief sweep through him.

"So," the doctor paused. "How has," another pause. "How has your last week been?" Dr. Fritz forced himself to ask the question he dreaded asking any of his patients. He had asked it with apparent interest, even a hint of innocence, but inside it was another story. As Ernie began to reply, Dr. Fritz was already slipping into a trance-like state of boredom, as yet another of his unbearably dull patients prepared to pour out their sob story of the week.

Dr. Fritz was deeply cynical. More cynical than any of his peers or his teenage sons. Six years of clinical training at Kings, followed by twenty-five years in under-funded psychiatric units around the country, had taken its toll. To make matters worse his wife was in the process of taking the children away from him, in a divorce that was so vitriolic it could have featured in an episode of Dynasty. Duncan, one of Dr. Fritz's old school chums, was his only friend outside work. Dr. Fritz was currently sleeping on a sofa in Duncan's living room. At the same time his soon to be ex-wife's personal trainer had taken over as head of the family, and was no doubt enjoying the comforts of the king-sized bed that Dr. Fritz had paid for. Who was he kidding? Duncan was his *only* friend. His colleagues at work, who did little more than nod at him in the corridors, could hardly be classified as friends. None of them seemed remotely interested in the doctor with the funny beard. Worst of all, it had become apparent that his wife had never liked him either. From the very start theirs had been a marriage of convenience. The prospect of marrying a successful doctor had pushed her into saying "yes" to a man she hardly knew and did not find remotely attractive. Or that was what she had shouted at him the last time they had spoken. All those years of wasted marriage, and even the kids were non-plussed with their Dad. No, correction, the kids did not like him at all.

"If only I'd listened to my mother," he thought ruefully, not even noticing Ernie pouring his heart out in front of him.

"Follow your heart, my darling. Do whatever

makes you happy. No-one ever ended up on the street by following their dreams," she had told him, but of course he had chosen to listen to his father. The man of the house, who surprise, surprise, was a successful Harley Street shrink. *"What did he know about anything anyway?"* he wondered. The world was run by men, wars were started by men, and he himself was the most pathetic example of a soon-to-be old man. Yes, women would probably do a far better job of running the planet. They certainly got things done.

As regular as clockwork Ernie dived deeper into his weekly sob story. The doctor screamed inwardly, without removing his mask of professional concern. He had got the, "No really, I *am* listening. I *really* care about your problems," expression down to a tee. Ernie regurgitated all of the minor disasters that had filled his life over the past seven days. A burnt carpet, feeling rejected by the man in the bookmakers, and the loneliness of not having anyone to talk to. Dr. Fritz had heard it all before, and not only from Ernie, but from all of his patients. A weekend course on quantum hydrology would have been more compelling, yet the good doctor held himself together and played the empathetic listener yet again.

10.15 a.m. Ernie's mood worsened as he moved onto his infatuation with Karen, his broken heart and the painful time that followed. Had Dr. Fritz not heard the same tales of woe so many times before, he might have listened. Instead, he fell deeper into his daydream, hoping his restless mind could entertain him a little more than Ernie. For the remainder of the appointment Dr. Fritz hoped to fantasise his way through a skiing holiday in Aspen, nodding occasionally but hardly noticing the man in front of him. As Ernie driveled on, a flashing red light appeared on the answer machine sitting only three feet away from Dr. Fritz's desk. He tried to keep his eyes on Ernie whilst half glancing at the machine. Miranda had left a message! He could make out her name spelt out in liquid crystal on the screen. In a poof of excitement both the white-capped peaks of Colorado and Ernie disappeared, as one hundred percent of Dr. Fritz's attention went to the answer machine. He was frantic to know what his wife had said. The masochistic portion of his mind hoped she had changed her mind, that she still loved him, and that somehow they could work it out.

"Even our pathetic excuse for a relationship is better than dying alone," he hoped, whilst at the same time loathing himself for his weakness. Besides, Miranda was far more likely to be complaining about the state of the children's shoes. Dr. Fritz had recently returned from a disastrous weekend of hill walking in the Pennines with his boys. It had been his best

attempt to forge some sort of a bond between himself, Sigmund and Eustis junior, but it had been a nightmare. From the moment they got off the train in Keswick the temperature had dropped, and the rain had poured down. The boys had moaned continuously, he had nagged them for the whole weekend, and finally his patience had snapped. Five minutes of ranting, with the boys staring back at him, looks of disgust on their adolescent faces, was enough to assure him they would hate him forever. *"My life is a mess."*

Ernie kept rambling, oblivious to the doctor's woes, and the good doctor did not hear a word he said.

10.25 a.m. Dr. Fritz backed further away from Ernie's verbal artillery assault, nodding robotically as his eyes looked straight through the little man.

"At last!" He found the slopes of Colorado again, and they looked as tempting as ever. Work was so boring compared to what could happen in his imagination. Dr. Fritz could bomb down black runs without fear of crashing, get smashed in the many Après Ski bars on the resort without the threat of a hangover, and meet an attractive divorcee on the slopes. Someone who appreciated him and wanted to share the happy times with a man she admired. Someone bubbly with jiggly boobs.

10.30 a.m. *"Thank God, over halfway,"* the doctor thought, as he glanced at a heavy grandfather clock standing behind Ernie. The image of the large wooden timepiece falling on top of his irritating patient flashed through his mind, and it felt good.

10.45 a.m. *"Why did I waste the better part of my adult life trying to please that woman?"* Dr. Fritz pondered, as he fingered his wedding ring morosely. He had not had the nerve to take it off.

"God, I am so weak," he muttered under his breath, then forced his mind back to those distant white peaks. The answer machine flashed persistently, and the babbling youth was too off-putting for the doctor's liking. There was no way he was going to return to Aspen right now.

"*I really should have listened to my mother,*" he thought.

"Become a psychiatrist," his father had told him. "It's nine till five with the chance to meet some of the maddest and most entertaining people alive." Thanks to his father's advice, Dr. Fritz had dreamed of rehabilitating hardened criminals, sitting face to face with remorseful mobsters, healing international pop stars of drug addiction and treating oversensitive artists' emotional scars. Unfortunately, it had not worked out that way, and now he was stuck in no man's land, ten years too far from retirement and ten years past any chance of a career change. Forced to listen to desperate, yet disappointingly dull people drivel on about their problems all day long. Meanwhile, Ernie kept ploughing through his story, his eyes ablaze and globules of spit flying across the desk towards the matted mammalian beard of his psychiatrist. His therapeutic catharsis well under way.

10.50 a.m. The doctor's stomach churned, though his mouth remained shut and his expression calm. *"Nothing like suppressing my emotions to get the stomach ulcers going,"* he mused. Taking advantage of a short pause as Ernie snorted into his handkerchief, Dr. Fritz clamped a hand over his mouth, trying to strangle a yawn.

"Is there anything new that you want to tell me today, Ernie?" The yawn escaped. "Anything positive? Or perhaps a little hopeful about your life?" He asked, a hint of sarcasm creeping into his. Ernie picked up on the doctor's lack of enthusiasm.

"Am ah boring you?" he asked, unable to hide his disappointment. He did not want to believe his psychiatric hero found him boring. That would be too much to bear.

"Yes! Unbelievably, you self-obsessed cretin," Dr. Fritz wanted to shout at him, but his conscience held him back. "I'm sorry, I didn't sleep so well last night Ernie. I think maybe we should call it quits for today, I'll see you next week. Okay?"

"Next week then," Ernie muttered, more deflated than when he had arrived.

"Next week."

Ernie hobbled to the door and once again struggled to open it. He did not dare to look back at Dr. Fritz for fear the shrink would crush his confidence again. He just shook his head, devastated that the man he had trusted had joined the long list of people who ridiculed him. After finally squidging through the wooden bear trap Ernie left the office with his head down and his gate sluggish.

The doctor did not have time to feel guilty and instead sprang to the answerphone with unrealistically optimistic butterflies fluttered around his stomach.

"Maybe she does want me back?"

Miranda's furious outburst forced him to step back from the answerphone.

"Eustis, you fucking moron, those kids were a mess when you brought them home. Both the boys were soaked, covered in mud, and as for the state of their shoes, they ruined the hall carpet. Can't you do anything right? I'm sending you the fucking cleaning bill. If you insist on using the children to antagonise me, I'll make sure you never see them again, ever!"

After that weekend in the Lakes it did not sound like such a bad offer.

o o o

Dr. Fritz sat alone in his office staring at the wall. He was not happy, and he knew it. His job was to help people to be happier and more functional, yet he had not managed to find happiness himself and his life was an archetype of dysfunction.

"Physician heal thyself," he whispered under his breath, shaking his head. He felt like a hypocrite. A hypocrite who had become trapped by the very life he had worked so hard to create. Trapped by his own desires for success, a happy family, and most importantly his desire to be loved. Yet, no matter how hard he had tried, none of it had made him happy. He was afraid he had failed at the game of life. "I am finished with this job. I want something else. I want to be happy," Dr. Fritz told himself, and he meant it. "I don't know what to do with my life. I'm lost and I wish someone would help me."

At that very instant, when Dr. Fritz became humble enough to acknowledge that he needed help, things began to change. He was not aware of it, but the wheels of his life started to spin in a different direction. Unseen forces he knew nothing about began to mould his destiny, and his future started to re-create itself ahead of him.

o o o

The following week Dr. Fritz was summoned to the hospital director's office. The director suggested he apply for early retirement. Rumours that he had been stalking his ex-wife had been flying around the department for months, and that was a scandal the hospital did not need. It was one of those suggestions that did not leave a lot of room for refusal, so Dr. Fritz took the hint and accepted it.

Initially the doctor did not adapt too well to retirement. What was he supposed to do all day? He made some pathetic attempts to get Miranda back. However, after the gym instructor had caught him hiding behind the herbaceous border, dressed as Batman, with twelve carnations in one hand and a box of chocolates in the other, Eustis Fritz finally saw sense.

o o o

Ernie spent the best part of a week getting over the rejection he had faced at the hands of Dr. Fritz. Ernie's fragile state did not leave much room for him to laugh at himself or shrug off disappointments. At a quarter to ten one morning, an NHS Transit van pulled up outside his home. As Ernie peered at the van through his net curtains, he felt a pang of regret. Dr. Fritz had been true to his word, perhaps he was not as unkind as he had seemed. Ernie hobbled into the hall and opened the front door, unaware of the terrible surprise that awaited him. As he unfastened the chain lock and opened his front door, his eyes came to rest upon a face he had hoped he would never see again.

"Holy shit! It's you!" he exclaimed.

"Erm, do we know each other?" the man replied. It was none other than Barry, the ambulance driver who had mowed Ernie down on his sixteenth birthday. Barry Clark had turned up at his door, van keys in hand, ready to drive Ernie to his appointment with Dr. Fritz. For a moment Barry's face remained benign and blank, as his brain attempted to put two and two together but kept getting the answer 'dunno'. Then the penny dropped.

"It's Ernie Manning isn't it?" Barry stuttered, as memories of his theatricals in court came back to him. Knowing he should apologise, but at the same time unprepared for such an unusual task, Barry scurried back to his NHS transit van and opening the passenger door, hoping this whole embarrassing situation would somehow disappear all by itself.

"This cannot be happening to me, like," thought

Ernie, and against his better judgement he hobbled down his driveway and into the van.

As they drove towards the hospital Ernie was silent, unwilling to waste energy in idle chit chat with the man who had nearly killed him. Barry hoped Ernie would say something, anything would have been better than the silent treatment, but Ernie did not open his mouth once. This made Barry increasingly anxious. He felt so guilty. He kept his speed down but although he was sitting behind the steering wheel, he was anywhere but. Barry's mind was all over the place.

It all happened so quickly. The dense woodland on either side of the ambulance moved past them in a blur. Barry failing to see the lorry reversing into the road ahead of them. Barry swerving. Ernie screaming, and the ambulance skidding to a halt a few inches short of the lorry's trailer. Enough was enough. Ernie had felt depressed for weeks, he felt weak, he felt like the unluckiest man in the world, but the adrenaline pumping through his slim veins galvanized him into action. Before he knew it, Ernie had taken the keys out of the ignition and was dragging Barry out of his cab on a quiet stretch of the A68. Ernie was not a violent man. He had spent his youth blending into the wallpaper of life so that no-one would notice him. So, it came as quite a shock when he snapped. Holding Barry by the scruff of the neck, Ernie looked him straight in the eyes and screamed.

"You ruined ma life once and ah am done with you and your crazy driving," he screamed with a rage he had never known. "All ah wanna do is smack yoose in the head with one of these," he continued, his face red with fury, as he slammed one of his crutches into the asphalt. "Tell your boss that ah don't want you driving me ever again. Ah hate you. You ruined my life and you never apologised. Ah want a taxi, and ah don't want you driving it. Understand?" Ernie's intensity surprised him more than Barry, but after years of avoiding confrontation it felt fantastically liberating.

Barry nodded meekly.

"If you ever see me again, like, cross the road," Ernie continued. "Walk away, and don't come anywhere near me." Still holding Barry by the shirt collar, Ernie peered into the dense woodland next to them. Then he hurled Barry's car keys into the brambles as far as he could. The keys flew high into the air and soared into the undergrowth, landing with a thud. "That'll keep you busy for a while," Ernie grunted. Barry nodded, too afraid to say anything. Satisfied he had made his point Ernie made his way to the psychiatrist's office alone.

TEN YEARS PASS

CHAPTER 12

Mirror, mirror on the wall

The last decade had not been kind to Ernie Manning. Without the guidance of his mother or Karen, a broken-hearted Ernie had spiraled downwards. He had begun a very unhealthy relationship with hard drugs in an attempt to forget his past and numb his hopeless future. Yet, no matter how much heroine he injected, he could never escape the pain of losing Karen. The first few hits were blissful, but their aftermath deathly, and he needed more and more to get half the hit. With nothing left for him in East Shields, he had sold his mother's house and bought a one-way ticket to Cambodia. There he blew the proceeds getting high, but this did not ease his pain. Wherever he wandered his problems and heartache went with him, eating him up bit by bit. That was when Ernie had crossed paths with Mickey, the Bouncer, and his life had never been the same again. Ernie and the Bouncer met in a bar in the Cambodian capital of Phnom Penh, in the winter of 1992. The Bouncer was keeping a low profile from Interpol. Interpol was interested in talking to him about various "misdemeanors" he had committed.

"These misdemeanors. I mean, really, they're nothing," Mickey had shrugged as he told Ernie of his past. "An alleged involvement in organising football riots, and the other, well, it's not even worth mentioning."

"What?"

"Plotting to make explosions, that's all."
Ernie raised his eyebrows.

"I mean, I've blown up a few buildings in my time," the Bouncer confessed sheepishly, "but I've never hurt an old person or a child," he added with more than a hint of pride.

"Oh, well that's okay. ah mean, what's a building or two between friends," Ernie had thought sarcastically, but decided to let bygones be bygones. The two men enjoyed each other's company, so why let a few past mistakes get in the way. After all, Ernie was not exactly an angel himself.

Ernie and the Bouncer became like brothers, spending the next six months dabbling in a variety of hallucinogens that the Bouncer insisted were prescribed for minor ailments in Asia. The Bouncer took a shine to the accident-prone youngster, taking Ernie under his wing, leading him astray and teaching him the subtle art of living on the wrong side of the law. Just as he had done with Karen, Ernie happily went along with it. For the second time in his life his quest for companionship was going to get him in trouble. Ernie was not a bad man, but he was a weak one, and the loneliness that had dominated his twenty years on earth, drove him to do whatever he could to keep other people happy. He forgot the promise he had made the day he was released from prison, and once again fell into the pit of criminality. It was a pit that he found difficult to climb out of. One that had a way of sucking him in and chaining him in darkness. The gentle kid from East Shields had to go, as Ernie became a tough guy.

After six mind numbing, brain rotting, soul destroying years, he and the Bouncer moved to London, broke.

Mission failed: Ernie was still pining for Karen and the Bouncer was still wanted by Interpol.

Back in England Ernie's troubles continued. Too many times he had woken up, not knowing where he was, sprawled unconscious in places that no one in their right mind would want to be. The street became his home. Part of him wanted to be rescued. Part of him wanted to die, and the rest, as usual, did not have a clue. The Bouncer eventually found Ernie work as hired help for a notoriously unpleasant businessman known as the Fat Man. Ernie was now twenty-six and not a pretty sight. He tipped the scales at nine stone, a stone lighter than he had been as a seventeen-year-old. He had a scruffy goatee beard with two bare patches on either side of his mouth. A pair of pin-striped suit trousers clung to his skinny legs, stained with a variety of substances, ranging from barbeque sauce to blood to vomit. An old pair of Hi-Tech Silver Shadow trainers which were two sizes too big, and a blue bandana pulled over his greasy mullet, topped off Ernie's fashion suicide. His capillaries were blocked and his skin discoloured, as he had moved around his body in search of fresh injection sites. He had started with his left arm, as any self-respecting junkie would do, and when that had packed in, he had moved on to his right arm, then to his armpits, his thighs, his wrists, his feet, and eventually his groin. He knew he would have to get off the hard stuff soon or he would die, but the hits were the only thing that dulled his pain.

"Ah'll get off it soon," he told himself, but never did.

Life had not panned out as Ernie had hoped, and the only person he could blame was himself. Sometimes he hated that shepherd for finding him alive.

o o o

The man was tall, well over six foot three, his shoulders broad and his face cruel. Taking a second to throw a look of disgust at his girlfriend, he grinned, then launched her against the kitchen wall, ignoring the thud of her head as he did.

"Ah'll fooking learn yoose," he roared, pots and pans clattering on the floor around them.

"Ow. Don't touch me," she screamed, lashing out with her fists and her feet but making no impression on the giant. He smiled sadistically as he held her hair in one of his huge hands, lining up the next punch. Karen's fighting spirit was strong, too strong. It meant she suffered more.

Karen had spent the last eighteen months living with a man who had revealed himself to be a monster. How had she ended up here? It had been ten years since she had been living in the Highlands with Rex, and it had all been going so well. Then Aunt Rose had died in the fire and her only blood relative had gone. It felt as if a pillar of stability had crashed to the ground, leaving Karen vulnerable and lonely. Before she had had a chance to get over Rose's death, she had given birth to two healthy twin boys. Rex had embraced the twins without hesitation, but he was an old man whose energy was waning.

An exhausting but rewarding year followed, with Karen too busy to dwell on thoughts of Ernie or Rose. Her twins filled those holes with love, tears, laughter and dirty nappies. Once she had finished breast feeding, Rex had offered to help find her a part time job, and she had started an apprenticeship as a car mechanic. Shortly afterwards, another blow struck the foundations of Karen's life. Rex was diagnosed with blood leukemia. Within weeks he had lost a short but peaceful battle with cancer. With no-one to take care of the children, Karen had to stop working and Rex's home was sold. His estate was passed on to a distant cousin, and Karen was given six weeks to move out. All of a sudden she found herself and her two babies with nowhere to stay.

Karen decided to head back to East Shields and try to build a life there. The next few years had gone surprisingly well. She had found a job in a launderette, rented a flat in a rough but affordable part of the town, and got the boys into nursery. It did not take long for Karen to become the manager of *Lisa's Launderette*, and a year after that the launderette changed its name to *Karen's Launderette*. With a loan from the bank she became the proud owner of her own business and it felt great. The boys did well, enjoying school and football, and her troubles seemed far behind her. She sometimes wondered how things could have been if

Ernie had not run away. It still felt wrong that they were not together, and no matter how many men asked her out, she could not say yes to any of them. Somehow that would be closing the door on the possibility that Ernie would come back.

When the boys were eight years old the Launderette hit trouble. Interest rates went up, a flood knocked out a dozen of her washing machines, and more people washed their clothes at home. The bank would not give Karen any more money to buy new machines, and she struggled to pay the rent for the Launderette and her flat. It looked like *Karen's Launderette* was going under.

That was when she met Dave. Dave knocked on her door one morning, with instructions to evicting her and the boys. The pretty brunette caught his eye, which was lucky for her, because he usually punched bad tenants down the stairs. He seemed so kind and honest when he offered them a roof over their heads.

"I can't let you live on the street. You can come and stay with me if you like? No strings attached. My last tenants just moved out and I have a spare room."

It was obvious that Dave had a thing for Karen, and although she did not feel the same way, she knew without his offer they would be out on the street. So, Karen and the boys moved in. Dave treated Karen like a princess, coming home with flowers and gifts. He was also very fond of with the twins, driving them to football practice four times a week. He insisted on giving Karen a loan so she could save her launderette. Karen succumbed to his charms and they got together. It was not long after that that Dave began to reveal his true nature, and it was not a pleasant one.

"Aaall mouth. Big tough Karen, aaall mouth," he slurred, as he squeezed her arms tighter in his steel like grip, pinning her against the wall. Dave was a weightlifter from Sunderland. Not a fair match for anyone, and certainly not a young woman worn down by months of his abuse. She should have left him after the first black eye. She should have known which way it was going to go. A man who got his kicks out of throwing people down flights of stairs was not going to change his spots. But if she left, where would they go? Who would be stupid enough to take the three of them in? If she stayed, at least the boys had a roof over their heads, that was the most important thing. Goliath, as one of her co-workers named Dave, controlled her financially. He would no doubt want his loan paid back as soon as she moved out, if he did not kill her first. If she left, not only would she be homeless, but penniless too. Karen loathed the excuses she made to justify his unjustifiable behavior, but being brave would have been easy if she had nothing to lose.

The beatings followed a predictable pattern,

usually coming after one of his drinking sessions. Goliath would stagger back from the pub, angry and belligerent. He would criticise her, put her down, anything to get a reaction. Karen would ignore him for a while, but if he was still able to stand up, he would follow her around the house, lashing into her with his wicked words. At some point she would tell him to piss off and go to bed. That was all he needed, and the violence would begin. Karen would fight back for a while, but eventually she would give up. She had to, if he killed her, what would happen to the boys?

Karen hid deeper and deeper within her own armour, existing rather than living. How her life had turned out shocked her. After her stepfather had left, she had vowed never to let another man bully her, yet here she was. She had always been the leader, the powerful, indomitable spirit who had done whatever she wanted, whenever she wanted. That Karen had to go.

The giant grabbed her in a bear hug. His breath stank of alcohol, gingivitis and hate.

"Ah gave her a slap to show her who's boss," he would tell his mates down the pub, treating the whole thing like a joke. Recently, things had taken a turn for the worse. Work had not been going well for Goliath and he took his frustrations out on Karen even more. This time she was not sure if he was going to stop.

"Ah'm sick of you disrespecting me, Karen. After all that ah've done for you," he slurred hatefully.

"She show's me no respect, no gratitude. She was nothing, a street rat with two kids who nobody wanted, and ah put a roof over their heads. She owes me." His twisted mind told him, as he clenched his fist into a ball. Another shove and the back of Karen's head crashed into the wall. Her world went blank, his words silent, and her eyes rolled upwards into her skull.

o o o

There was not a day that passed when Ernie did not think about Karen.

"Ah wasted my only chance to be happy, like. Why was ah so stupid? Why didn't ah tell her ah'd been arrested?" If Karen had been around everything would have been better. Ernie would not have blown the proceeds of his mother's house on drugs and wild parties with people he did not know, nor care about. Who was going to save him now? No one, but in a masochistic kind of way that was okay, because he no longer wanted to save himself. No, Ernie was dying a death of a thousand cuts, and that was what he deserved.

He had tried to find Karen many times, but life as a heroin addict was hard enough, without trying to track down a missing person at the same time. From time to time he would stumble into a phone box, call directory enquiries and ask for the number of a Karen Walsh, probably living in Newcastle, but his efforts came to nothing. There were hundreds of Karen Walsh's in England, and he did not have an address. After a while the heroin won, and Ernie gave up.

"The good times never last."

o o o

"He's a bloody idiot," screamed the Fat Man, his voice booming from behind his desk, spittle flying from his mouth. "Why the hell did you send Ernie Manning to meet Babyface? That moron could not organise a piss up in a brewery, so why the hell do you think he's qualified to deal with the biggest smack dealer in South London?" The Fat Man wiped his brow with a silk handkerchief. "Bloody hell, he's a pissing liability. The only reason I haven't killed him yet is because one day he'll make such a good patsy. What the hell were you thinking, Mickey?"

The Bouncer kept his eyes down and his mouth shut, slowly edging away from his employer. He was the only one of the Fat Man's original men who had survived a string of bloody purges over the years, but he was not sure he was going to survive this one. "Cat got your tongue?" growled the Fat Man. "When is he supposed to pick up Babyface?"

"Erm, about now, Guv."

"What! Now! Oh shit. If all this goes wrong, I'm going to make you pay for it," the Fat Man threatened, as the vein on his forehead pulsated angrily, sucking hatred from every part of him and throwing it in the direction of the Bouncer. In a flash, the Fat Man sprung from behind his desk and moved across the office with surprising speed, grabbing the stocky thug around his neck. The image of the bloated billionaire threatening a man who looked like he could murder a herd of bull elephants, was absurd. However, the Bouncer was terrified, and with good reason. He was in a spot that nobody in their right mind would want to be in, and his only way out was to apologise, and sort this mess out. Even that might not save him. Taking the Fat Man on was not an option. The Bouncer's own certain victory in a one-on-one street fight with this tub of lard would be short lived. Even if he managed to get out of the building alive, he would be on the run forever, constantly looking behind him, never knowing when the hit would come. No, it was wiser to eat humble pie, say sorry and reverse his mistake. Playing the hero with the Fat Man only got people killed. "Exactly what was going through your tiny mind when you hired Ernie Manning?" the Fat Man demanded again, his face inches from the Bouncer's.

"There was no-one else, govner," he replied in a thick cockney accent, his eyes searching for somewhere else to look. Anywhere but into those pale, blue eyes. "Charlie's in the Scrubs, Mad Paddy's gone AWOL, and every other sod's got the flu. I fought just vis once it would be okay. I didn't this meeting was so important to you. Sorry Guvna, it won't 'appen again."

"To bloody right it won't, because if you don't sort this out, nothing will be happening for you, ever." The Fat Man stared right through the Bouncer and slowly released his grip on his neck. Then, true to his unpredictable nature, he flicked a switch in his crazed mind and calmed down unnaturally fast, and the vein went back into hibernation.

"'E's not playing wiv a full deck. No way," thought the Bouncer, noticing a pungent smell fill the room. The Fat Man's relative calm was more intimidating than his rage, and the Bouncer felt no safer for it. Then it dawned on him, the smell was fear, his fear. *"I gotta get out of here, for good,"* the Bouncer thought, moving backwards towards the door.

"This job is sensitive, if Manning cocks it up, I won't get the information I need. If I don't get that information, then I won't make any money, and that will really ruin my day. *Comprendé*?" he turned his back on the Bouncer and took a step away from him. Then he stopped, placing an index finger on his lips, as if he was pondering something of vital importance. Spinning around the Fat Man grabbed the Bouncer's neck once more. "Now go and get that bloody weirdo off the job before he screws this whole thing up," he whispered in the Bouncer's ear. "In fact, I don't want Ernie Manning on any job ever again. I want him out of the way, permanently. Do you understand me?"

"Yes, Guv. Consider it done." The Bouncer knew what was good for him and left.

o o o

Squinting at his Mickey Mouse wristwatch Ernie sighed with boredom. He was alone, kneeling in the corner of a deserted warehouse in east London, well hidden behind a stack of wooden packing cases. His face was contorted, unable to hide his disgust at the stench of rotting garbage that filled the building. An array of discarded junk littered the warehouse; rusted food tins, Coke bottles filled with soil and smashed up pieces of wood. Green slime from the copper roofing above dripped down the damp stone walls. It was dark inside, with the only light coming from small window slits high up near the ceiling. Babyface was late for his meeting, and Ernie did not like it when people were late. Things went wrong when people were late, and when someone as heavy as Babyface was late, it could only spell trouble. These were the times Ernie felt the most ill at ease. The times when he was left alone with nothing to do but spend time with his thoughts. Staring into the darkness from behind a half-smoked Benson and Hedges, he cupped the cigarette close to his nostrils, partly masking the smell of excrement around him.

"Two hundred quid is peanuts. This job's not worth it, like, ah can smell it," he moaned quietly to himself, wheezing as he drew the comforting fog into his lungs. His thoughts, as they so often did, went to Karen. He scrunched his eyes closed and tried to remember some of the small details. The way she smelled. That knowing look she used to give him which melted him every time. Her disapproving looks as he blew his nose on one of his old handkerchiefs at the dinner table. It was so long ago he was not sure if he truly remembered anything, or if he was making the whole thing up in his head. It had been over a decade since he last saw her. Over ten years since he had ignored her advice and been arrested by the store detective. He could still remember how cold it had been lying in the slush that covered the hard pavement in Newcastle city centre. It was sad that he remembered that so vividly, yet so little about Karen herself. Ernie knew he had been head over heels in love with her, but the feeling itself was long gone.

    A Glock nine millimetre semi-automatic pistol was strapped to his protruding rib cage. The lethal handgun looked quite out of place attached to this unlikely hit man. Ernie's crutches lay beside him. He had done a few jobs for the Bouncer in the last few months, all of which lay well on the wrong side of the law. However, he was confident that his *Day of the Jackal* disguise would keep him out of the hands of the authorities. The police were not in the habit of stopping and searching a disabled man hobbling away from the scene of a crime. As far as Ernie knew, he was the only handicapped hit man in Britain. He was also the only hit man who had not killed anyone and had no intention of ever doing so. He had kept this piece of information to himself. Hit men who were averse to violence did not tend to get a lot of work. Exactly how long Ernie could remain employed and also avoid hurting anyone, he was not sure. However, sooner or later his boss would find out the truth, and Ernie would have to disappear very fast.

    Every few minutes he would move his right hand from the floor, unbutton his pistol from its holster, and inspect it with an expression somewhere between horror and intrigue. He would then cock it, check the chamber was clear, release the pin, replace the magazine, and button it back up in its leather pouch. He never kept a round in the chamber for fear of a misfire, which with his history of bad luck, was probably very wise.

o o o

When Karen came to, she was alone in Goliath's flat. Her sadistic partner had no doubt made his way to the pub to boast to his friends of his recent heroics. Had the cold hard tiles of the kitchen floor felt more pleasant against her cheek she might have stayed there. Instead, Karen picked herself up off the floor with arms that felt so weak they struggled to respond to her commands. Too dizzy to stand, Karen sat on the corner of one of the steps that lead from the kitchen to the living room. Her expression was one of disgust. Disgust at what had just occurred and disgust at herself for being so weak. The kitchen was dark, with a glimmer of light coming from an exposed bulb hanging in the hall. Its lampshade smashed long ago in a similar fight. Karen touched her lip with a finger and winced,

"Ow!". Her head was throbbing, and one of her ribs cried out in protest every time she breathed but thank goodness she was still breathing. It was hard to tell if the pain or the humiliation hurt the most. No, it was not, the humiliation did not hurt it killed her. Leaning a hand against the wall she edged herself onto her feet and shuffled towards the bathroom. Her first instinct was to look at herself in the mirror, but she could not bring herself to do so. Before she could stop herself, she threw up into the toilet.

Sitting on the fluffy, pink toilet seat in the windowless loo of the tenement she called home, Karen prayed she would not have to go to the hospital again. She could not face the looks of the nurses as they nodded politely, unconvinced by her lies. In the last few months Karen had been so clumsy; walking into doors, falling down the stairs, and tripping over the boys' toys. At least, that is what she had told the concerned staff at the hospital. Silly her, it had been her fault, not the boyfriend who punched and kicked her whenever he was having a bad day. The nurses and doctors had offered her help.

"There are places you can go, you know? You can take your children with you. You'll be safe." They had told her with kind concern, but she would not take the help. He would find her, and then he would kill her. With his connections and history, the authorities had no way of keeping her safe. She so wanted to leave Goliath, but where could she go? Without him she had no money. He was clever, he had lent her the cash to save her business and had insisted on becoming a silent partner. A partner who controlled the finances. So, really, it was not *Karen's Launderette*, it was his. She had her plans to leave him, and over time had stolen a few hundred quid from the launderette and his wallet, but it was not enough. Her money was controlled by him. Her life was controlled by him. It was hopeless.

"Please someone, get me out of this. No-one deserves to live like this. No-one," Karen wept as drops of blood splattered onto the floor from her nose, or her head or her mouth, it was hard to tell. "Please, please, please, God if you exist, please help me." She had never felt so desolate in her life, never pleaded out loud to a God she suspected had long given up on her, but what did she have to lose?

Karen held a wad of toilet paper over her nose and mustered up the courage to stand in front of the bathroom mirror. Looking at her reflection, she instantly regretted it. A tired, ugly, wrinkled old woman stared back at her, with a hollow, defeated look in her eyes. Her hair was all over the place, her jawline swollen, and one of her eyes was closing up. She looked like she had been hit by a train.

"*I used to be so strong. I could hold my own with the toughest kids in the North East. What has happened to me, and why do I still miss you Ernie?*" she thought. Karen had firmly believed that time would heal her heartache, but it had not. Yes, she did not think about him as much, but the longing to see him again had not changed. *"So much time has passed, and I still miss you like crazy."*

Her gaze went to the razor blade perched precariously on the bathtub next to her, and a dangerous thought crossed her mind. But only for a second. She knew she could never desert her boys. Shaking her head to send her dark thoughts away, Karen looked at the Mini Mouse watch strapped to her wrist and a single tear ran down her cheek. If Goliath knew who had given it to her he would have smashed it long ago.

It was seven o'clock. The boys would be back from Karate class soon. So, Karen cleaned herself up, put on more makeup than she wanted to, and went into the kitchen to cook them their tea.

"Enough is enough," she told herself, gaining strength from the rage she felt inside her bones. He had not touched the twins, but they were getting older, and it was only a matter of time before his short fuse was lit by them. She was not going to let that happen. *"That was the last time,"* she vowed, placing a sharp kitchen knife into her handbag. If Goliath hurt her again, it would not be her who was taking a trip to hospital.

Karen wondered if he was somewhere else hurting somebody else. She did not know. All she knew was how she hated him. How she hated her life. And at the bottom of all of it, how she hated herself. *"Ernie, Ernie, why did you leave me?"*

o o o

Ernie's daydream was ended abruptly by the sound of heavy footsteps heading in his direction.

Smash.

The rotten door at the far end of the darkened warehouse was kicked open and three men entered. Daylight streamed into the warehouse, making Ernie more exposed than he would have liked. He peered out from behind the packing cases, trying to see without being seen.

"*Shit, ah was told one man, not a whole crew, like,*" he gasped, a knot of fear gripping his stomach. The Bouncer had assured him this was a simple job. Babyface would be alone, he had said, and Ernie could handle it. Clearly Babyface had broken his word, and now Ernie was in a world of trouble. Shuffling further into the corner, he studied the three thugs who had walked in. Sure enough, Babyface was there, but despite his name he was well over six foot two and was flanked by two other tough guys. Ernie recognised them from bare knuckle fights in the East End and was sure they had not been hired for their people skills. No, these guys meant business.

"Where is he? Hey, where the are you, Fat

Man?" Babyface shouted, his voice commanding more respect than his age entitled him to.

"Oh shit." This guy scared Ernie, and his friends scared him too. *"Ah have to get out of here,"* he thought in a panic. *"Ah can't handle three lunatics on me own, like."* Ernie took a minute to think and came up with a cunning plan. *"Put down some covering fire, pin them in a corner, and get out of here as fast as ah can."* He knew it was a terrible plan, but it was better than sitting in a darkened corner waiting for them to find him.

Ernie reached for his holster, unbuttoned it quietly, wrapped his bone-thin fingers around the Glock, and counted down the seconds in his head.

"One elephants. Two elephants. Three elephants," he thought, cocking his pistol quietly.

Before Babyface, or either of his henchmen, could react to the faint click, Ernie struggled to his feet, closed his eyes, and sprayed bullets in their general direction as quickly and brutally as he could.

Blam.
Blam.
Blam.

As he emptied the magazine, the pistol kicked back in his hand again and again, his eyes clenched tightly shut.

>Click.
>Click.
>Click.

In a panic, Ernie shoved the Glock down the front of his trousers. A searing pain hit him as the hot metal burned through his underpants.

"Ow, ow, ow," he shrieked, and ripped the pistol out of his trousers, throwing it into his backpack. Without looking back, Ernie grabbed his crutches and headed for the door as fast as they would carry him.

o o o

His work for the day done, the Fat Man leant back into his reinforced leather chair and stretched his arms upwards, enjoying the satisfying clicks of his spine. Once again, he began to think about the Tibetan monk and the possibility of finding some relief from his racing mind. These days it never seemed stop. His plans for retirement had not advanced one bit. There was always something important happening that he could not trust anyone else with, particularly not Tarquin. His son had not exactly shown himself to be someone worthy of trusting. No, retirement and finding peace would have to wait.

"I don't have time for such nonsense," he chastised himself. *"I've got a business to run. Besides, I know a better way to relax."* Pouring himself a large brandy he gulped it down, hardly tasting the priceless liquor. Then two more followed in close succession. *"It could be worse,"* he sneered, glancing at the clock sitting on the corner of his desk. *"I could be impotent."*

Four thirty.

"Plenty of time," he thought, as he pushed the buzzer on his intercom. He spoke with a voice which was softer than usual.

"You lads can go home now. I won't be needing you untill tomorrow. Okay?"

The five security guards secreted throughout the building all replied identically, one after another.

"Okay, boss." PUT IN REASON FOR THE FAT MAN NOT RETIRING AS HE PLANNED 10 YEARS BEFORE

It was not like the Fat Man to let his guard down. With the number of enemies he had, an around the clock, elite team of ex-special forces bodyguards was necessary. Yet, from time to time high-level criminals needed a bit of space, and right now was one of those times. The Fat Man leaned back in his chair once again and allowed a broad smile to spread across his face.

"Finally, some time on my own."

Swinging himself out of his chair, he walked over to one of the seven huge mirrors that hung around his office. It was an impressive Victorian room. Its ceiling decorated with heavenly cherubs and mythological, dragon like creatures. As was becoming his habit, he stood alone facing one of the oversized mirrors, but this time he refused to be negative. This time he was going to have a little fun. Turning sideways the Fat Man examined his profile, sucking in his huge gut as best he could.

"Nearly seventy and you've still got the magic," he declared, though he was not as convinced as he would have wanted to be. Marching over to his state-of-the-art surround system, the Fat Man fumbled to find the track he was looking for. Then he pressed play…

"Oooohhh you can dance, you can jive, having the time of your life. Ooooohhhh see that girl, watch that scene, you are the Dancing Queen…"

The unmistakable voices of Abba erupted from four speakers suspended from the ceiling.

"Ahhh, my babies," he cooed, and walked back to the mirror. Looking himself up and down the Fat

Man nodded and...

Then he started to boogie.

Despite his ample dimensions and age, he was quite a mover, strutting his stuff like a teenager as he got into the groove. He twirled, he moon-walked, he jived, but despite being sorely tempted, he held himself back from trying to do the splits. It did not stop there. As he boogied his way from one mirror to the next, he started to undress. Casually casting his silk tie to the floor, followed by his shirt, but only after he had swung it over his head a couple of times. By the time he was halfway through the song, the Fat Man was dancing in nothing but a pair of colossal red knickers and a gigantic matching bra. Richard Branson could have made a hot air balloon from his lingerie alone.

...*"You're in the mood for a dance, and when you get the chance, you are the Dancing Queen, young and sweet only seventeen. Dancing Queen, feel the beat from the tambourine oh yeah..."*

The music blasted, and the Fat Man sang along with all his heart, massaging his stomach and caressing his neck and thighs seductively as droplets of sweat flew from his body with every dance move. He was quite literally, having the time of his life...

"*Dancing Queen, ahhhh ahhhh ahhhhh, ahhh ahhhhh...*"

Finally, the music faded, and he flopped back into his chair with a huge grin, sweating like a water buffalo.

"I'm not used to all this exercise," he chuckled. It had been far too long since he had treated himself to a private dance, and it felt great. So wonderful to escape the constant pressure that weighed him down. Lighting up a Havana, he closed his eyes, took a deep puff and relaxed. *"If only my mother could see me now,"* he thought, exhausted. Then, like a flick of a switch, the Fat Man fell fast asleep. Soon he was snoring quietly, looking a bit like one of the cherubs flying high above him.

CHAPTER 13

The Bunker

A steel encased air raid shelter. 45 yards below ground. An unknown location. Surrey, 1997.

Kevin the Terrorist looked nervously over his shoulder as he struggled to unlock the riveted steel door as quickly as he could. It had been over thirty-five years since he had been half beaten to death by the Fat Man, and his panic attacks were not getting any better. Within minutes of stepping outside the safety of his bunker, Kevin would break into a cold sweat, fighting the panic attack that lurked beneath it. At last the lock clanged, and with sweat dripping from his forehead he used all of his weight to push the creaking door open. The fifty something Accounting Assistant for Crawley County Council winced as the hinges screeched against the concrete floor. As soon as there was room enough for him to squeeze through the gap, he disappeared into the darkness within.

As Kevin made his way down the spiral staircase, his light footsteps echoed in the silence. At the bottom of the stairs he stopped and entered a seven-digit pin code into a small white keypad next to an inner door. The lock whirred and clicked, and finally he could relax. The living room, if you could call it that, was pitch black. Kevin took out a ten pence lighter from his pocket, stumbled over to a corner of the room and lit a candle. The candle's feeble flickering light was swallowed up by the large room, but for Kevin it provided more than enough light to see. Kevin's bunker was a lonely place, with no sofa, radio or television. Indeed, it had nothing that might offer him any sort of comfort in the long winter evenings. The air in his makeshift home was damp and metallic. There were for obvious reasons, no windows, which did nothing for the ambiance of the place. Although it looked more like a medieval prison than someone's home, to Kevin it *was* home. The aneurism that had damaged his brain had left him without many of the needs that ruled ordinary people's lives. He felt happier in darkness than in sunlight. He did not appreciate home comforts, and the fewer people he came into contact with the better. This Spartan approach suited him well. He liked it that way.

Already the relief of being hidden away from the dangers of the world was calming him. The bunker may not have been the Savoy, but it offered a tremendous security which eased his paranoia somewhat. Kevin's eyes adjusted to the darkness, and as he scanned the room he allowed himself a satisfied smile. His meticulous, twice daily eye-training programme had enabled his irises to adjust to the dark three times faster than an ordinary civilian. This made him awfully proud.

At first glance Kevin looked like a regular middle-aged guy. He was five foot nine, had mousy hair, a plain and unremarkable face and wore a mid-range Marks and Spencer's suit. However, if one took a closer look, there was a lot more to Kevin than met the eye. He was extremely fit for his age, had a straight back and buttocks that could crack a walnut with ease. Another remarkable trait with Kevin was the stutter the Fat Man's fists had left him with. This stutter made talking about anything that was not absolutely necessary painful, to say the least. His living arrangement was also far from mainstream, but then again, nobody knew where he lived.

Standing next to the living room was a storage cupboard stacked with assault rifles, tubs of Semtex, hundreds of tins of baked beans and fifty copies of the

SAS survival handbook. Kevin's unconventional home was not connected to the National Grid. It had its own internal electricity generator that could generate around five kilo watts of electricity an hour. This was not to save money, he could easily have paid for the bunker to be wired up to the mains, but he believed the less he had to do with anything official the better. It was bad enough that people knew where he worked, he did not want them knowing where he lived as well. It was safer that way. When the war came, the National Grid would be one of the first things to be knocked out, and most of the world would be without electricity. He on the other hand, would have more than enough fuel to survive for a decade without venturing out. Yes! He would be one of the only humans who had practical experience in how to survive without the luxuries most spoilt mortals took for granted. This old air raid shelter may not be the most luxurious of places, but it had its advantages when it came to the aftermath of World War Three.

Kevin took off his suit jacket and trousers, removed his shirt and tie and proceeded to fold each item with meticulous precision, before placing them on an empty shelf. He then disappeared into a side room and five minutes later Kevin, the Terrorist, emerged wearing camouflaged combat trousers, knee length black assault boots and a green mesh vest of the type that many Middle East Dictators favour. Plastered onto his head was a bright red beret with his personally designed insignia on it; a picture of a kangaroo and a human hugging.

"Ahhh. It's good to be home," he panted, fumbling around the sink to pour himself half a glass of water. The living room had a grated metal floor, beneath which hundreds of cockroaches had made their home. As Kevin walked over to the candle which was welded to a solid steel table in the corner of the room, he could hear the clicking black bugs scattering into cracks in the wall. A normal person would have hired Rentokil to dispose of these unhygienic guests. To Kevin they were a source of protein which might one day keep him alive, and he was happy to have his little clicking friends living so close by.

The walls were lined with hundreds, perhaps thousands of books, many of which smelt of mould. There cannot have been a conspiracy theory on the planet not covered in some shape or form by this library of paranoia. As well as being a practical way to while away the long winter evenings, Kevin believed the books offered further protection from a thermo-nuclear attack. Not only could they absorb the power of the shockwave, but they would reduce the negative impact of high radiation levels too. Or at least he thought he had read something like that somewhere.

Most of the books were full of nonsense a ten-year-old would have laughed at, but Kevin had read every single one more than half a dozen times and believed every single word they said. One would have been forgiven for thinking this unusual man was all alone in the world. It had been years since Brenda had left him, and the bunker had not a hint of the feminine touch. Indeed, it was not a place any self-respecting woman would want to visit, let alone live in. Yet, although Brenda was long gone, Kevin was not all alone in the world. He did indeed have a friend who lived alongside him in the depths of his cave. He was Kevin's only real friend in the world. A friend who was absolutely loyal and unwavering in his adoration for this extraordinary man. A friend who did not say a great deal but loved Kevin from the bottom of his heart. A friend who surprisingly was covered in soft, golden fur. Sitting in an empty bookshelf only inches from the table was something that could have been mistaken for a large rat but was not. Kevin stroked the animal's hairy back and whispered tender words of kindness in his ear.

"There you g… g… go my friend," he cooed as he scratched the back of the animal's neck. "Who's been lonely whilst Daddy's been away? Not to worry, Daddy's back and he's very pleased to see you." As Kevin petted him, Skippy the stuffed kangaroo, sat quietly on the bookshelf and did not say a word, but that did not mean he did not understand.

Most evenings Kevin would take out one of the old books from his library and read it to Skippy, but tonight he was not in the mood for reading. No, tonight he had something far more important to occupy himself with. Pulling his wrought iron chair closer to the table, he moved a little nearer to the candle and started to fumble with a small recording device. Finding the record button...

Click.
Kevin started to talk.

"28th March 1997, a secret location, England." He invariably started this way, imagining himself to be a cross between James T. Kirk and John Rambo. A hero dedicated to leading the human race when this immature species finally self-destructed. "S... s... someone once said if the Third World War was fought with nuclear bombs, then the Fourth World War will be fought with b... b... bows and arrows, and it was a wise, wise man who said it. You see, I know the Prophecy my little friend, I've had the d... d... dreams," he stuttered, his voice strained and hoarse. "S... s... swelling populations, p... p... pillaged natural resources, hurricanes, crop failures, diseases, volcanoes, billions will die." He paused to remove a dried cornflake from

Skippy's coat. "There you go young soldier, all spick and span," he beamed at his best friend in the whole wide world, and then continued. "W.. w… when will it happen? I am not p… p… privy to that information? But it will happen, and I will see the signs, because I am ready." Beads of sweat flowed down his forehead and two wet patches pulled his shirt closer to his soaking armpits. "International tension will at some point escalate, as good for nothing politicians, intent on clinging to p… p… power refuse to give in to the demands of the people. Then it will all get too intense and, b… b… bang! If you're not wearing factor one million sun block you are going to have a really b… b… bad day. You know what I mean Skippy?"

The kangaroo said nothing.

"N… n… nuclear holocaust, courtesy of some rogue Arab state who has managed to buy enough plutonium from disgruntled nuclear scientists with nothing to lose. Or some deluded President who wakes up in a bad mood and decides to p… p… press the red button. Don't be disheartened, this won't be the end, Skippy. Some of us will survive. A privileged few. People like you and me, who give up the privileges of leading a normal life, and spend our time underground, training.

There will be a new b… b… beginning, a new era for the planet. Out of the ashes common people will find renewed strength. You will be one of those people,

I mean animals, I mean persons, you know what I mean, Skippy," he never quite knew how much his friend understood and did not want to offend him. The kangaroo continued to say nothing. "But anyway, the world will be a very different place. It will be more like times of old, and we will enjoy that. Won't we S… S… Skippy?" he looked to the kangaroo, as if expecting an answer.

"B… b… brave men and women will strip naked and wrestle for supremacy, like magnificent Greeks in ancient times. There will be tournaments to decide who is the g… g… greatest warrior, who is worthy to lead humanity, and from the c… c… chaos of c… c… combat a ch… ch… champion will emerge." Images of the boyishly handsome Jason and his Argonauts flashed through the Kevin's mind. "Yes, someone with intelligence, someone invincible in combat, yet wise, a man of the people. D… d… do you know who that champion will be, Skippy?" Kevin stared into the distance poignantly. Then, wiping a tear from his eye, he looked dreamily at the stuffed toy kangaroo who continued to remain silent. "Ah yes, always the silent one, silent but strong. You know something my friend? *I* will be that Champion, and you will sit b… b… beside me as I rule the world. Together we will rebuild humanity the way it was m… m… meant to be. We will create a perfect society, an orderly and fulfilled society.

Yes, we will create a society based on the sturdiest of foundations. A society built on love, truth and c… c… compassion." He turned and looked his best friend straight in the eye, "and anyone who opposes us will be eliminated."

o o o

As soon as Ernie had escaped out of the back of the warehouse, he made his way to the nearest pub and poured enough booze down his neck to kill a small bison. Too drunk to make it back to his dingy squat, he had ended up sleeping it off in a skip in Hackney. Just another typical day in his mess of a life.

Waking up with a tongue as dry as a badger's bottom, and a head that felt like jelly, the young Geordie panicked in the darkness.

"Ah've been buried alive!"

Kicking off the top of the metal skip, he gasped with relief, sucking in lungfulls of fresh air. *"Thank the Lord."* He was still alive and very much above ground, though exactly where he was, he had no idea. Looking up and down the street, it was the same as any other back street in north London. Rubbish and bin bags were strewn around, rusty drainpipes oozed their contents onto graffiti covered brick walls, and not a soul was to be seen. Ernie shrugged and clambered out of the metal skip that had been his bed for the night, cursing the smell of rotting fish that had smeared itself all over his trousers. As he pulled his legs over the edge he lost his balance.

"Damn it", he swore as he fell, knocking over a dustbin lid which clattered to the ground. Lying on his stomach he looked at his bloody hands and grimaced. Tiny bits of stone were stuck under his skin, and blood was running from a cut on his wrist. It was nothing serious, just another little nail in the coffin of suffering that he lived in.

"Perhaps ah'll just lie here and bleed to death, like?" he thought morosely. *"Someone might find me, but if ah'm lucky, they might not."*

His thoughts continued.

"Ah'm no use to anyone, like."

"Better off dead."

Struggling to his feet Ernie perched on the corner of a dustbin and began to role a cigarette. It was painful, but he persisted, spurred on by the calming effect he knew it would have.

As he took a deep drag from his roll-up, a man dressed in a blue janitor's uniform appeared from a doorway in one of the nearby buildings. Ernie watched the man push a trolley of bright yellow, phone books towards him.

"Morning," muttered Ernie, looking at the

ground, but the man did not reply. He pushed the trolley right past Ernie, parked it and then threw the stack of Yellow Pages into the container. Without saying a word or even acknowledging the homeless man's existence, he walked back towards the doorway from whence he came. As he did, one of the Yellow Pages that was perched on the top of the skip, slid and dropped to the ground next to Ernie. The janitor turned his head, shrugged and pushed the trolley back inside. For no reason at all Ernie bent over to pick up the phone book. By co-incidence, it covered the Tyne and Wear region of the UK but was three years old.

"That's strange. A Yellow Pages for Newcastle in the middle of London?" He thought, his shaking hands struggling to leaf through the pages, but something drove him to scan each one. There was nothing out of the ordinary here, and he felt stupid for bothering. However, on page two hundred and fifty-five Ernie's eyes rested on something he never dreamed he would ever see. *"Oh my God. It can't be,"* he gasped, as his cigarette fell from his open mouth.

o o o

"Aw bollocks," the Bouncer snarled under his breath, shaking his head as he surveyed the carnage in front of him. Three bodies lay within five feet of each other, caked in blood, entrails poking through holes in bullet ripped clothes. Babyface and his two thugs would not be causing anyone any trouble anymore. The Bouncer sat down on an old packing crate and put his head in his tattooed hands. 'Love' and 'hate' cradling his cranium, as he tried to work out what to do next. He remembered his last conversation with the Fat Man. There was no escaping it. This time he really was dead meat.

"'Ow the 'ell am I going get out of vis one?" he wondered. It did not take a rocket scientist to work out who was responsible for this monumental cock up, but the Bouncer was the one who was going to pay the price for it. The Bouncer dabbed one of the bloodstains on Babyface's corpse with his pinky finger. It was almost dry, which meant the assassin, or rather that screw up of a junkie, could be miles away. *"Well, not miles, 'e's not exactly Ben Johnson."* Without wasting any more time, the Bouncer stepped over the bodies of Babyface and his two cronies, made the sign of a cross on his chest, and jogged outside into the fresher air.

o o o

"Karen's Launderette. The best in Byker! Call us for all your laundry needs, both big and small."

Read the advert on page two hundred and fifty-five of the Yellow Pages. Below the text was a photo of a woman who was the spitting image of...

"Can it really be you?" Ernie rubbed his eyes and took a closer look. "It is! Oh my God, it really is!" he gasped, his voice jumping two octaves. Two minutes ago, he thought he had been buried alive and now he was looking at a black and yellow photograph of Karen. She was holding a laundry basket under one arm and giving a thumbs up with her other hand. Ernie's vision was far from twenty-twenty, but although he could see she was smiling for the camera, her eyes were full of pain. Or was he imagining it? "Oh My God! After all this time!" Ernie sang, still not believing what he was seeing. Here was a picture of Karen, and not only that but an address of where she worked. He had given up all hope he would ever see her again, and now it looked like she was working only a few hundred miles away. The address was in Byker, one of the rougher parts of Newcastle, and if he hurried he could be there by nightfall. He could find her, explain everything, and they could be together again.

Ernie ripped the page out of the phone book, looked at it once more, folded it, and tucked it into his back pocket. He then hobbled towards the end of the street with all the purpose a hung-over addict with crutches can muster. Then his steps slowed.

"Who am ah kidding, like?"

"She must have found someone else by now."

"Ah'm a junkie. Why would she take me back?"

The doubt that had crippled Ernie's life tried to defeat him once more. *"Ah'm so different to the man she fell in love with. Ah'm a wreck, an addict. A good for nothing worthless piece of shite,"* he told himself. His hobbles slowed and his head bowed a little more with every step as a deep sadness filled his heart. Soon he had come to a halt, and then he turned around. Making his way back to the unlit cigarette still lying on the ground beside the skip, he picked it up, re-lit it, sat down, and did what he had done best for the last few years. Ernie Manning put his head in the sand. *"Ah'll only get me heartbroken again,"* whispered the voice in his head.

Chapter 14

Mission failed

"At last," the Bouncer muttered, as his gaze rested on Ernie's crippled figure sitting alone on a bench smoking a cigarette. It had taken Mickey half a day to find Ernie and he was relieved to get to him before one of the Fat Man's other goons. Ernie looked relaxed, not at all concerned that he would soon be wanted for three murders. As the Bouncer moved closer, Ernie got up and hobbled away. The Bouncer followed, keeping a safe distance behind him, waiting patiently to get his chance. It did not take long.

Ernie turned into a side street and the Bouncer followed. Lurking in this dark, back alley was a leather clad man with a tattoo of a straight flush inked across one of his cheeks. Ernie nodded a greeting to the man and handed him a pile of crumpled fivers. The drug dealer gave Ernie a small packet in return.

"Idiot. Three dead bodies and 'e wants to get stoned," thought the Bouncer as he crept towards his prey. The dealer saw the Bouncer approaching, so Mickey raised an index finger to his lips. The drug dealer got the message and said nothing, slowly backing away from Ernie.

"Oi! Twinkle Toes! Didn't you know drugs are bad for your 'ealth?" the Bouncer's voice boomed in Ernie's ear. "And I'm an awful lot worse than drugs."

Ernie whipped around just in time to take a stinging left jab to his face.

"Holy shit, man," he whined, really backwards, lifting his hands to protect his face. This did not work as Ernie deftly blocked the Bouncer's second punch with his chin and skillfully took a head butt to his nose. Falling to the ground, Ernie gasped for breath as his broken beak squirted blood all over his Silver Shadow trainers. The Bouncer turned to face the drug dealer.

"Piss off, unless you want some of the same?" he snarled, and the dealer ran off. The Bouncer then turned back to Ernie, a look of bewildered rage on his face. "Bloody 'ell, are you trying to get us both killed?" he shouted, fear and anger fighting to gain control of his voice box.

"Calm down, man," Ernie replied, dabbing his lip

with the back of his hand. "What's with all the anger, like?"

"Anger? I'll give you anger, you stupid twat. The Fat Man boiling the two of us alive, that's anger," the Bouncer continued, his body shaking with rage.

"Take it easy man. This isn't my fault. You said there was only going to be one guy, and then three of the bast'ads turned up," Ernie protested, holding up his hands to keep the Bouncer at bay. "What was ah supposed to do, like?"

"What were you supposed to…" The Bouncer shook his head and went to kick Ernie, but his foot stopped short, bullying was not his style.

"Calm down Mickey. There's no need for violence."

"Really? I wish you'd thought that back in the warehouse. Tell me Einstein, 'ow are we going to get out of this one?" asked the Bouncer, composing himself a little.

"Come off it, man. So, ah pissed off a few want-to-be gangsters. They were tossers, like. All tooled up, but no place to go, if you know what ah mean?" Ernie grinned through blood-stained teeth, blowing smoke from an imaginary pistol. "Anyways, you should be more worried about hitting like a girl," Ernie smiled. "Sneaking up behind me like that. What's wrong Mickey? You lost your touch?" he goaded, spitting a bloodied tooth into his hand.

"With friends like you, who needs enemies?" seethed the Bouncer, as he pulled Ernie to his feet. Before the Bouncer could blink, the young Geordie threw a right jab at his nose.

"Ah shit," Mickey swore, staggering backwards.

"Ah've still got the magic, Mickey. Now we're quits," Ernie declared triumphantly, wiping the blood from his own mouth with his sleeve.

"Bloody 'ell, Ern, if we wasn't friends I'd." The Bouncer then gripped his nose with both of his meaty hands and cracked it back into place. "Aaaargh, fack! That hurt."

"What's the problem, like? Babyface and his two mates weren't there to talk. Ah had to put a few rounds down and make a run for it." His face lit up, "Ah'll tell you what," he said, "why don't ah buy you a beer?" Ernie suddenly looked guilty. "Actually, you'll have to buy us one, cos ah don't reckon ah'll get the two hundred quid from the Fat Man for that job, and ah'm tapped out."

The Bouncer shook his head in disbelief.

"You 'ave no idea what you've done, Ern, do you?" he asked, a puzzled expression on his face. "You was supposed to take that Babyface to the Fat Man, without laying one of your oily fingers on 'im. Not blow 'im and his pals to kingdom come."

Ernie's face dropped.

"What? Ah put down some covering fire and scarpered, that was all. Ah didn't hurt anyone, like," he replied.

"Ern, you killed three of the toughest guys in North London. I've seen 'em. They're as dead as doornails. They're jam bread. Pushing up daisies. You know?"

"Oh, no," said Ernie, as the reality of what he had done started to sink in.

"D'you know any good clairvoyants? Cos that's the only way we're going to get the Fat Man what 'e wanted from Babyface. What was you thinking of, Ern?"

"Ah just wanted to get out of there. Ah had no idea ah had shot them, like. Ah usually miss everything."

"Well, even a broken clock tells the right time twice a day. We're in big trouble, cos the Fat Man himself has sent me kill you," the Bouncer frowned.

"Does that mean you're going to kill me?" Ernie asked sincerely.

"No, I am not going to kill you. But I want to," he smiled. "When the Fat Man finds out about Babyface, he's going to kill me," the Bouncer exclaimed. "In fact, that's bollocks, he's going torture both of us to death in some warehouse in East London.

You weren't meant to kill 'em, Ernie. That snotty kid had stuff in his head that the Fat Man wanted."

"Ah had no idea, like. Ah didn't mean to hurt anyone. Really."

"Well, it's too late now Rambo. God, I need a drink," mumbled the Bouncer, "come on. Let's go somewhere and enjoy our last few hours still breathing." Ernie nodded and the two friends headed to Brick Lane to forget their troubles for a while.

o o o

"I want them both dead, and I don't want to see your ugly mug you until they are," the Fat Man spat at the man standing in the doorway of the House of Horrors. The man was unnerving at the best of times. He was a tall, thin Hitler look-a-like, whose lack of anything close to a conscience made him invaluable in a world where violence always had the last word. The vein on the Fat Man's forehead throbbed with every word he shouted. "Jesus, fuck, I don't need this kind of stress, Spider."

"I'm getting too old for this," the Fat Man thought, but chose not to share this insight with his employee. The Fat Man was furious. Not only had Ernie Manning murdered one of his most lucrative business partners, but Mickey, his righthand man, had betrayed

him. Spider remained silent, unphased, knowing his skills as a hunter and assassin were too valuable for the Fat Man to dispose of, no matter how angry he became. Spider slowly drew his long tongue across the front of his train track braces and sneered in a way that exuded evil rather than resentment. He was glad to be hunting real prey, but his blank expression revealed nothing of this. Not even the Fat Man could read Spider, and Spider liked it that way. When the Fat Man had given Spider all the information he needed, the hunter hissed, nodded twice and left. In the course of the whole conversation he had not uttered a single word.

o o o

By one o'clock in the morning, the unlikely pair had found a resting place for the night, perched against the bar of an illegal drinking den in Old Street. Ernie and the Bouncer sat opposite each other, nursing their pints and putting a brave face on their dire situation. Ernie felt terrible. He had done some foolish things in his life, but he was no killer. Yet, now he was. He had murdered three men in cold-blood and dragged his best friend into the middle of it all. What would his mother have said?

The Bouncer was more philosophical. It was no

surprise that Ernie had got him into hot water. From the first moment they had met in that seedy bar in Phnom Penh, Mickey had sensed the air of disaster that hung around the skinny redhead. The Boucner had found it quite appealing and his protective instincts had compelled him to take Ernie under his wing. The Bouncer should have been furious, but they had been through a lot together, and now, close to death at the hands of some anonymous hitman, he could not help but chuckle. It was impossible not to forgive his disaster-prone friend. His tongue loosened by the booze, the Bouncer broached the subject of their imminent deaths.

"Ernie, you realise after tonight we can't ever come back to London? Ever. We've got to get out of 'ere quick-smart and start off somewhere new."

Ernie glanced down at his hands, playing with his fingernails nervously, and then looked his friend straight in the eye.

"Mickey, ah need to show you something." Taking out the crumpled Yellow Pages advert from his back pocket, Ernie unfolded it and showed it to the Bouncer. Mickey took the piece of paper from Ernie's hand, and read it, slowly.

"Is this who I think it is?" he asked.

"Yes," Ernie whispered, "ah thought ah'd never see her again, like, but then this appeared out of nowhere. Some random bloke dropped it in front of me."

"Facking 'ell, Ernie, this is a miracle. I mean, what are the chances?"

"And one more thing Mickey. Ah haven't told you this before, but this whole thing is not just about me and Karen. We had a kid together."

"Jeez Ernie, a little sprog! That changes the whole caboodle."

"Ah've never met me kid. Karen left us when she was still pregnant, like. Ah divn't know if the kid even knows it's got a dad."

"What are you gonna do?" asked the Bouncer.

"What can ah do? Look at us, ah've got nothing. She's probably married by now anyways. We were kids, like, and she was way out of my league, even back then."

"Yeh, but what if she's in trouble? What if your kid's in trouble? What if they need your 'elp?" the Bouncer asked. "It's not easy bringing up a kid on your own, and she might not 'ave found someone else. Don't you think you owe her the chance to make up 'er own mind about that? I mean, I know you're a facking disaster waiting to happen, but maybe she's got a soft spot for disasters," the Bouncer said tenderly.

"You don't know Karen, she can look after herself better than most, like," Ernie replied, shaking his head. "Ah divn't think me turning up, in the state ah'm in, is gonna do her any favours, like. Ah'd only bring her and the kid trouble."

"Come on Ernie, you got to try and find 'em. I mean, what 'ave you got to lose? She lives in Newcastle. She runs her own Launderette. I mean, 'ow 'ard can it be to find 'er? Let's face it. You're probably going to be dead in a few days anyways."

"Ah don't think ah can take any more bad news, like. You know? If she tells me to sling me hook, or worse, if she hates me, it'll break me in two."

"Listen," the Bouncer's voice hardened, and his head crept closer to Ernie's face. If you're going to die, you want to see them before you go. I know you think you've made all these mistakes in your life, and maybe you 'ave, but who hasn't made mistakes? You've got a chance to make it right. Someone up there is giving you a second chance. You should bloody well take it, my friend." The Bouncer's words hit Ernie hard.

"What if he's right? What if Kazza's in trouble. What if ah can help her?" A flame of courage started to burn inside the young Geordie. *"Ah can do it. Ah can see her again, and if she doesn't want me, well, ah'll deal with that if it happens."*

"Since ah found that advert, Mickey, ah think about her every second, like, every second," Ernie said, tears welling up in his eyes. "She probably won't take me back after all these years, but you're right, Mickey, ah've got to try."

On that fateful night, in a dingy bar in East London, with a dozen hired assassins bearing down on them, Ernie made a choice. With his back against the wall and his best friend in front of him, he made the *right* choice, not the easy one he was so used to making. That choice freed the butterfly of goodness from the cocoon of chaos that had blighted his life, and in the space of one drunken conversation everything changed. The forces of nature began to spin to a different melody and Ernie Manning had something to live for again.

"All right, that's decided, like," Ernie gulped, "Ah'll find her, and if she'll have me, ah'll take her and the kid somewhere fit for a Queen. Falaraki, Ibiza, ah don't care, there are lots of paradises in this world, and most of them are only an EasyJet flight away." As he spoke he started to believe his own words, his mood lifted, and he gazed into the distance as if communing with a god who had long deserted him. "If ah can get myself straight and win her back, then the world will be my oyster and Karen my little clam."

The Bouncer stared at Ernie, utterly bemused.

"What the hell," he offered, lifting his pint for a toast. "Everyone's got to dream, and we'll both be dead within a week.

"Cheers!"

"Cheers!"

"It's decided then. I reckon we've got to stick together on this one Ern. Besides, 'ow are you going to survive without me?" chuckled the Bouncer. "We'll both head up to Newcastle tomorrow, first thing. I'll ride my bike up the A1, and you get your arse to Kings Cross and take the train to Newcastle. The Fat Man's gravitational pull is not as strong up North, so we can buy ourselves some time whilst we figure out what to do next. Do you know of any decent pubs there?"

"Course ah do. The Cradlewell in Jesmond is a good place."

"Okay. I'll see you in the Cradlewell tomorrow night. Don't get followed, alright?" The Bouncer's face became stoney. "We'll have to be careful Ernie, Newcastle is not going to be the first place they look for us, but it'll be on their list, alright? The Fat Man's going to pay a lot of money to some seriously 'ard people to find us. These're not the sort of people you want after you, and if they catch us, it's not going to be good. I've seen what the Fat Man does to people who betray him, and it's not pretty."

The two friends gave each other a manly hug, complete with back pats, to reassure each other there was nothing remotely homosexual about their show of affection. Then the Bouncer took out two fifty-pound notes and put them into Ernie's palm. "Remember, we only use cash from now on. This should cover your train fare, and get yourself some new clothes, because you stink like a pig," he said, winking. Ernie stuffed the notes into his trouser pocket. The two friends left the bar and went their separate ways, disappearing into a night they feared they might never survive.

o o o

As Ernie walked the ancient streets of London, his body began to tremble with fear. The waves of heroism he had mustered up with the help of his friend the Bouncer faded, leaving him feeling vulnerable and alone. As a rule, Ernie enjoyed the quiet solitude of the small hours, but tonight there was something eerie about the London streets. A thick fog had descended, and the air was full of unknown terror and foreboding. All Ernie wanted to do was stagger back to his squat and collapse, but not tonight. The Fat Man would be gathering his evil forces, and most likely there were already a couple of hoods waiting there for him, eager to put a bullet in the back of his head.

It only took the Fat Man to say the word, and hundreds of snitches and petty criminals would be climbing over each other to give him the information he wanted. The Fat Man punished mistakes, but he also rewarded help most generously. Yes, the dogs would be out, and Ernie had to make sure they did not pick up his scent. Anonymity was going to be his closest ally from now on, and apart from Mickey he was on his own. He could not return to any of his old haunts and he could not contact any of his so-called friends. He had to assume that everyone he trusted would be willing to put a bullet in the back of his head, just to win favour with the Fat Man. Ernie figured he had to find somewhere rougher than usual to sleep. So, he headed into Weaver Fields, a park far enough from his squat to offer some sort of safety.

Lying himself down on a wooden bench Ernie tried to make himself comfortable. It was easier said than done. He found some old newspapers and a discarded coat which he used as a makeshift mattress, but he felt as if he was lying on a hard Guillotine block, waiting to be chopped. Lying all alone in the darkness he felt the world had once more turned against him. It was not a new feeling, he had felt that way for most of his life, but the stakes were higher now. Staring up at the night sky he shivered. Memories of him and Karen staring into the night sky crept into his mind.

"Ah love you Karen Walsh. Ah love you and ah'm coming to find you," he whispered and promptly passed out.

CHAPTER 15

On the Lamb

When Ernie woke, he was gripped by a fear that threatened to paralyse him. It was five o'clock in the morning, and a deluge of paranoid thoughts ran through his head as his bloodshot eyes scrambled to recognise where he was.

"Where the hell am ah?" His mouth was as rough as a Puffin's borrow, his head throbbed, and his body was shaking uncontrollably. An ache in his chest told him one thing. *"Ah need a fix."* Throwing off the newspapers and the coat which had failed to keep him warm, he fell off the bench, landing hard on the ground.

"Ow," Ernie grunted, but without getting up he began to search his pockets for cash. He found the crumpled fifty-pound notes in his back pocket and it all started to come back to him.

"Oh shit, ah'm meant to be at Kings Cross. Ah'm meant to get the train to Newcastle and find... Karen." Yesterday's conversation with the Bouncer, and the plan they had hatched seemed ludicrous in the cold light of day. He had talked his old friend into following a pipedream. A pipedream that could only end in failure. *"Ahm', so stupid, like. Ah've no chance of getting her back,"* a voice in his head told him. *"Less than none,"* another replied. How could a severely hung-over junkie avoid assassination, catch a train to Newcastle, track down Karen, and then convince her he was the answer to her problems? It did not make sense.

Looking around frantically, Ernie squinted to see if he was alone, but it was too dark. This was somewhat reassuring, because if he could not see anyone, then none of the Fat Man's goons could see him. However, it would be getting light soon, and then he would be vulnerable. He would not know the difference between an ordinary Londoner going about their business and a hitman, and he would not know when the hit was coming.

The morning was absolutely still, with not a breath of wind in the air. Had he not been in so much danger he might have enjoyed this quiet hour of solitude before the chaotic awakening of the people of London. Taking the crumpled advert out of his back pocket, Ernie took a moment to look at Karen's face for the last time. They had been so good together. Those few summer months in 1985 had been the happiest of his life. Fumbling to find the box of matches he kept on him at all times, Ernie opened the pack, took out a match and thought one final thought.

"Ah'm sorry Kazza. Ah can't come after you. Ah'll only hurt you." He hated himself for thinking it, but it was true. He had enough money to get to Newcastle and the Bouncer had his back, but what he did not have was self-belief.

"Ah can't get rejected again Karen, ah'm too weak. It'd kill us, like." he mumbled in despair. "Sorry." A single tear dropped onto the yellow paper, thudding to a halt and staining the paper an ochre hue. Ernie turned his back to shelter from the wind and struck a match. The sulphorous, yellow flame touched the corner of the only object still binding him to his true love. "Goodbye Karen," he sobbed, as the flame was drawn hungrily towards the dog-eared advert. "Just two kids having some fun, but it wasn't meant to be…

The good times never last."

o o o

Put in Yellow pages from a few years ago.

A gust of wind came out of nowhere and blew the flame out.

"What the?" muttered Ernie, shaking his head before striking another match. The phosphorous tip growled as its white heat searched for something to devour, but before he could light the paper in his hand another gust of wind blew him onto his back. The box of matches flew out of his hands, somehow landing almost ten yards away from him. "Ouch," Ernie yelped, as his head thudded against the hard ground for the second time that morning.

o o o

As Ernie sat on the grass of the deserted park, his head throbbing from overindulgence and the bang it had just had, a figure appeared out of the darkness and stood over him. This was it. This was the end. One of the Fat Man's goons had tracked him down and was about to finish his pitiful life. There was no need to find Karen anymore. A part of him felt relieved.

"Just get on with it," he said, without even glancing at the figure.

"Get on with what?" said a voice that took Ernie back to his childhood. Ernie turned his head and saw it was not a hitman but a woman standing beside him. A woman dressed in black who looked like his mother.

"Is that you, Mam?" Ernie whispered, rubbing the back of his head.

"Yes, Ernie my love, it is."

"It can' be. Ah saw you fall," he replied.

"Ah haven't got a lot of time," she interrupted. "There are things ah need to tell you. Important things." Ernie moved to get up but could not.

"What are you doing, Ernie?" Babs asked.

"Hallucinating by the looks of things. It can't be you. Ah saw you fall. God, ah killed you with my stupidity"

"It *is* me, and ah did fall, but it wasn't your fault," she reassured him, her body shimmered slightly. Ernie relaxed a little.

"Ah've missed you, Mam. Ah really needed you. Ah've done some bad things, really bad," he sobbed.

"Listen carefully. Ah know this whole thing is weird, but you've got to trust me. Okay?"

"Okay," Ernie sniveled.

"Ah know you've done some foolish things, but there's a bigger picture that you don't know about. Life is different to what we think it is."

Ernie did not compute.

"Can you remember when we used to play poker at home, in the evenings when it was raining?"

"Yeah, ah remember."

"Well, life's a bit like a poker game. We get dealt our cards, and we do our best to play them. Some people get a full house on the flop, and other people get a five-two off suit, but you know something, Ernie? We have to play the cards we've been dealt. Life is different to what you think it is. A successful life is not about what you achieve, what job you get, or how successful you are. It's about who you are and who you become. If you leave this world a better place than when you arrived, you've played your hand well. If you become a better, kinder person, you have done even better. If people knew that who they are is much more important than what they achieve, this world would be a better place."

Ernie kept staring at her.

"Are you getting any of this?"

"Erm, kind of?" he lied. "No, not really."

"Remember when ah used to tell you bedtime stories? Ah used to tell you about the Knights of the Grail. You must remember?"

"Ah remember, Mam. I always wanted to be Lancelot"

"Well, here's the thing: You can be. Even though you were born on the wrong side of the tracks, you can be noble and help people just like Lancelot. Everyone has the chance to be good and do good, no matter how far they've fallen. You don't realise this. You think you are worthless. You believe what the thoughts in your head are telling you. In fact, you are ruled by them.

But you're lucky. Why? Because life has not gone your way. You've hit a brick wall, and it is screaming:

'For God's sake stop! Do something good before it's too late, you miserable bastard.'

For you this wall is drugs, misery, a broken heart. For some is losing all their money, or their friends," Babs shimmered again. "Ah haven't got a lot of time, Ernie. You've hit about ten brick walls, and you won't stop headbutting them. Can't you see they are a sign that you need to change course? You can move towards love, or keep giving in to fear, it's up to you. And you know what? Love is often the hardest choice.

Ernie, listen to me. The woman you love is in trouble. She needs you. And you need her. If you don't go to her, you'll both suffer for it. You have to follow your heart, you have to do the right thing and do it before it's too late," Babs's voice was full of compassion for her wayward son. "You weren't born by chance, Ernie. You were born for a reason. If you do the right thing, then you *will* succeed. If you keep going and don't give up."

"Ah don't understand, Mam. How? Look at me!"

"Ah want you to start living your life as if you can make a difference. Ah want you to help a woman who needs you more than you know."

"But how am ah ganna be able to face her, like? Ah'm a mess, full of holes from the smack."

"You need to be brave and honest, Ernie. You have no idea what a big difference one person can make. What a difference you can make. It's not your fault, you have got lost. Most people are lost. But you've got me coming back from the dead telling you, and not many people get that!

You need to wake up and learn that those thoughts in your head telling you terrible things are thoughts, nothing more. They're not real. They are like ghosts. It's like you're living in a dream."

"More like a nightmare," he mumbled.

"But you are one of the lucky ones. You've hit that brick wall, so you've got good reason to turn around."

"How does she know all this stuff?" Ernie wondered, rubbing his head again.

"Mam, are you an angel now?" he asked.

"Sort of, ah'm one of your guardian angels, my love. Ever since ah laid eyes on you, ah loved you completely, and that doesn't end just because ah died. Ah'm sworn to watch over you and help you when ah can, but ah haven't got any more time right now. "You need to sober up, get clean and follow your heart, before it's too late." Babs' light body started to shimmer and fade. "Ah have one final question for you, Ernie," she said.

"What is it, Mam?"

"What are you going to do?"

Ernie looked away.

"Ah don't know. Ah don't think ah can do it," he whimpered. "Ah screw things up the whole time. Ah'm no more than a piece of shite, that's all! Ah rob people for smack, just to get through the day. For pity's sake, ah killed me own mother."

"Ernie, my love," Babs replied, swelling with love. "You didn't kill me, it was an accident. You've not got time for regrets, just learn from your mistakes. You're a man now, and you have far more courage than you think. Whatever choice you make, ah will love you. Be strong, Ernie, you must be strong. Your boys need a father..."

Then, with a final shimmer and a flash of white light, the vision vanished into thin air and Ernie passed out.

o o o

For the second time that day Ernie woke up in the park. Rubbing his blurry eyes, he looked around expectantly for any sign of his mother. The light of the morning sun, which itself was not quite visible, made it easier to see that the park was deserted.

"*Did ah make that whole thing up?*" he wondered, because right now nothing seemed quite real. Placing a hand on the arm of the park bench Ernie stood up, stretched like an old alley cat, yawned loudly and scratched his behind. Whether the vision was real, or he had imagined the whole thing, Babs' words had done their job. He felt a steely resolve that had been absent for years, perhaps since his days in prison. It was inside him and it felt good. His life could no longer be about Ernie Manning and his problems, he had his mission and he had to get on with it.

"Ah've gotta get me-self to Newcastle," he whispered quietly, and headed in the direction of what he hoped was Kings Cross, with a spring in his step and steel in his heart.

o o o

The young Geordie hobbled up the carriage of the London to Edinburgh express train, his crutches clasped tightly in his unwashed armpits. The carriage felt horribly claustrophobic, and a stream of haunting thoughts chased him down the train. Everyone he passed was a potential threat, and even old ladies had a certain air of menace about them. The first twenty-four hours of a manhunt were the most dangerous, and if Ernie could survive those, he was in with a chance. But his chances were not good. Both he and the Bouncer had crossed a line, and their lives could never go back to how they had been. Whatever it takes, was the only attitude that would get Ernie out of this one alive. Whatever the risk, this was a journey he knew he had to make. A journey spawned from love, from the stars, from destiny's own dark belly. It was a journey that could end one of only two ways. Success or, well, he did not want to think about the other one.

o o o

Now that Ernie was sitting down in the relative comfort of his Intercity 125 reclining seat, he had a chance to notice how bad he felt. He was used to feeling like roadkill, but the previous night's binge on top of the heroine withdrawals, felt unbearable.

"You need to sober up, get clean and follow your heart," his mother had told him only hours before, but rather than heeding her words, he stumbled into one of the train toilets. Delving into his pockets Ernie took out a small metal box. In it was a syringe, a length of rubber tube, and a blackened tea spoon. Opening the box with shaking hands, he looked at the brownish-white powder and frowned. It was not a pleasant dilemma. If he was going to find Karen he could not get high, but if he did not get high, he would not be able to get himself off the train and find her.

Striking a match and melting the greyish white powder in a teaspoon, he tied the rubber tube around his arm. "Sorry Ma. Today's not the day to go cold turkey, like," he muttered to himself, as he injected the lethal venom into a protruding vein.

o o o

The Intercity 125 pulled into Newcastle Central station. Ernie crashed onto the platform with the stealth of a hippopotamus, and then disappeared into the Saturday afternoon shopping crowds.

Bump.

"Sorry mate, ah didn't see you there," Ernie apologised to the small Japanese man he had collided with. The Asian tourist apologised profusely; unaware he had donated his wallet to the scruffy looking Geordie with a limp. "Sorry, Mam, but desperate situations required desperate measures," Ernie whispered to himself, looking skywards. He was now better equipped to get on with the serious business of finding Karen.

Ernie's next stop was a run-down charity shop just outside the Station. He had been there once before with Karen, but did not remember. He left his old, stinking clothes in the changing cubicle and came out wearing a green and white shell suit, a new pair of Silver Shadow trainers that miraculously fitted him and a pair of fake navigator sunglasses.

"Looking good," he commented, giving the thumbs up to his reflection in the shop window. However, he could not ignore the butterflies flapping crazily in his stomach. Karen's Launderette was so close, he might meet her in fifteen minutes. It was the most terrifying moment of his life.

The Victorian terraced houses of Byker felt familiar. Single mothers hung out their laundry, skinny children stalked around in gangs, and old men muttered to themselves as they headed to the bookmakers. Karen's Launderette was just a couple of minutes away and Ernie needed a drink. He pushed his way through the double doors of the Bell and Whistle public house. The doors half crushed him and then spat him out.

"What is it with me and doors, like?" he mumbled.

Two whiskeys later, he went to the toilet, renewing his ongoing battle with another set of wooden doors.

"No rest for the wicked," he grunted and headed for the urinals. As he splashed his face with the bitterly cold water from the filthy sink he collected his thoughts. "Here goes nothing," he whispered. The eyes that stared back at him from the broken mirror were steady and determined.

Ernie found himself standing in front of a small laundry with paint peeling off the window frames. The front door was battered by the boots of customers carrying laundry baskets under their arms. Laminated onto the front window in bright purple ink were the words *Karen's Launderette*. A surge of emotions tried to send Ernie headfirst in the opposite direction.

"Calm down, Ernie, breathe," he instructed himself then crossed the road and push open the glass door. The small Launderette was no different to every other Launderette. It had a row of industrial washing machines whirring in unison, and an old man in a tweed cap watching his clothes tumble around in an old dryer. Apart from the old man the launderette was empty. Ernie limped up to the counter and caught sight of a pair of women's legs in the back. His heart fluttered, was it Karen?

"Excuse me". Cough. "Erm, e-excuse me," he stammered, and the legs turned around and walked towards him.

"Yeh, how can I help?" the launderette asked casually.

"Oh."

"Are you okay?" smiled a plump blond girl. "You look, disappointed, pet."

"Er, well. Ah guess ah am. Ah'm looking for Karen, ah believe she owns this place? Ah'm an old friend of hers, from East Shields," Ernie told her.

"Oh, Karen's got the day off, pet. But she lives only fifteen minutes away, you can probably catch her at home," the friendly girl replied. She scribbled a map with Karen's address on a laundry slip, turned around and walked to the back of the launderette.

Ernie was scared. Walking into the shop had been bad enough, knocking on Karen's door was another matter. Who knew what would meet him there? Was she married? Would she remember him? Would his long-lost love want him, hate him or have forgotten all about him?

Thick rain clouds were gathering above, and an ominously dark shadow cast itself over the streets as Ernie quickened his pace. Focusing on a street name ten yards away, he realised his eyesight was not what it used to be. In fact, his whole body was not what it used to be. He glanced at his discoloured hands, covered in scars and burns, and once again his courage left him.

"How can ah see her when ah look like this? Ah

look like a tramp," he thought. His worries ended as two young lads smashed the passenger window of a Toyota Corolla in front of him. Accompanied by the piercing wail of the car alarm, one of them grabbed the stereo, the other a handbag from the front seat, and they both ran off in different directions. *"Screw how ah look. Ah need to get her oot of this place, like,"* Ernie thought and continued with renewed determination.

CHAPTER 16

The End of Ernie

By the time Ernie found Karen's home, early evening was setting in.

"Ah never was good with directions. Oh well, it's now or never," he thought. Before he rang her doorbell, Ernie crossed the street and stopped in front of an abandoned corner shop, studying his reflection in the darkened window. He straightened his hair and examined his face with the intensity of a fourteen-year-old about to go on his first date. Licking his handkerchief, he smoothed out his eyebrows and patted down his hair. Then he blew his nose and shook his head with a faint smile, as he remembered how his handkerchief used to annoy Karen. Satisfied he was as presentable as he would ever be. He fumbled around

in the pocket of his shell suit.

"Gotcha!" he mumbled as he took out a small, brass-plated hip flask and took three long swigs from it. "For courage," he added quietly.

"You'll need it," his mind added, and he shivered with fear. As if echoing his trepidation, a crack of thunder almost lifted Ernie off the ground, shattering what was left of his composure. Huge drops of rain began to pour onto the pavement, and Ernie was soon soaked through. *"Oh bollocks. I guess making a good impression is out the window,"* he thought and hobbled away from the corner shop cursing the clouds above him.

White as a sheet, Ernie rang what he hoped was Karen's doorbell and waited for a reply.

Nothing.

"Come on, please be in," he whispered, bouncing rapidly on one foot.

Still no answer.

"Come on, come on, *please* be in. Ah can only do this once."

As Ernie was about to walk away, the door flew open, and all of a sudden he wished it had not. A giant of a man stood in the doorway, reeking of booze, staring down at the drowned rat on the doorstep. Ernie's heart sank. Clearly this was not the right house.

The Goliath of a man was an awesome sight, so

tall his head pushed up against the door frame, he had muscles that bulged out of a skin-tight Sunderland football shirt. His face was stained burgundy from the chronic state of anger he had been in for forty-five years. His neck carried scars so horrific that whatever had inflicted them would have had no problem killing an ordinary man five times over. Goliath turned to shout back to someone in the house.

"Oi! Have you invited anyone over?" he bellowed.

"No. I'm not expecting anyone," replied a faint woman's voice from within.

"Then who the fook are you?" the giant snarled, turning to face Ernie and poking him in the chest.

"Ah'm Ernie, ah am sorry, I rang the wrong..." he muttered, stepping backwards.

"Ah was watchin' the football, so you'd better have a good reason for botherin' us on a Saturday afternoon. Ah don't like being bothered when ah'm watching football," he growled at Ernie.

Ernie could actually smell the violence coming off him.

"Ah have got to get out of here," he thought, waved apologetically and started backing down the stairs. Then, before the thug could come up with any more witty insults, a bruised face peered out from behind one of his biceps. It belonged to the most

beautiful woman Ernie had ever seen. A door in his heart that had been shut years, flung open. It was her. It was Karen. It was Karen, and she was as beautiful as ever.

Ernie could not quite believe how lovely she was. Slightly battered, but still divine, exactly as he remembered her. Then two small boys appeared behind their mother, looking almost identical. Their mother clutched them protectively.

"Oh no, just what ah thought. She's got herself a new family. She won't be wanting me," thought Ernie as his heart shattered to pieces.

Suddenly out of nowhere, he could hear Babs' voice,

"Ernie, you must be strong, your boys need a father…"

"Boys! She said, boys! It all makes sense," he thought, and before he could stop himself, Ernie opened his mouth.

"Ah don't believe it, ah have got two wee boys," he whispered to himself.

"What did you say?" Goliath demanded.

Ernie had no idea what to do next, but what came out of Karen's mouth limited his options somewhat.

"Ern, oh my God, Ernie Manning! Where the hell have you been? I thought you were… That you must be…" She stopped herself, staring at him in disbelief. Here he was, after all these years, her true love standing on her doorstep. He looked quite well, she thought, slightly battered, but still divine.

"Holy shit, ah've got twins," was all Ernie could stammer. He studied the two soon-to-be ten-year-old boys, not quite able to believe his eyes.

"You what?" snarled the giant. He had now decided to do some serious damage to this drowned rat on his front doorstep. The expected, 'Who's this tosser?' followed by the 'He's my ex-boyfriend who I thought I'd never see again but has returned to rescue me'- conversation never happened. Instead, the thug discarded formalities and punched Ernie over the small garden hedge.

Smunch.

Goliath's punch was like no other Ernie had ever got in the way of. The old adage, 'the bigger they are the harder they fall,' may have been true when uttered from the lips of Bruce Lee. However, in this case, 'the bigger they are the harder they hit,' was more to the point. Ernie's crutches remained in the doorway, while he landed a few feet away in a puddle on the pavement.

Sploosh.

It was only the shock of landing in the icy puddle that kept Ernie conscious. Goliath did not waste any time gloating over his handy work and strode towards Ernie with his fists and his teeth tightly clenched. Before he could get his hands on the skinny bloke lying in the puddle, Karen pushed past her sadistic boyfriend and ran up to Ernie, placing her hand gently on his back.

"Ernie. You've gotta get out of here," she whispered in his ear, "he's a bad man, a really bad man." Karen knew what was about to be unleashed, and there was no way her Ernie could survive it.

"Cut it out, Dave. Go back inside," Karen pleaded to Goliath as he was walking down the steps towards them. "He's nobody. Just a guy from years ago, and he hasn't done anything to you."

Ernie groaned, spitting a mouthful of blood into the puddle, staining it pink.

"Do you mean that, about me being a 'nobody', like?" he asked quietly.

"Of course, I don't. I've never forgotten about you, you plonker. Now get out of here," she whispered back.

The thug did not bother to look at Karen before smashing his forearm across her face. Then it was the twins' turn to face his wrath. Together they rushed towards Goliath, wrapping their little arms around his legs as they tried to protect their mother.

"Stop. Stop. Stop," they screamed.

Goliath laughed and kicked them off, roaring at them to go back into the house. The big man's attention now turned to the little man on the ground.

"You knocked on the wrong door at the wrong time. You little shit," he snarled, but Ernie did not care.

"She hasn't forgotten about me. After all these years," he thought triumphantly. *"Ah'm going to get her back, and no muscle head's going to stop me."* A surge of courage coarsed through his body, galvanizing his wasted legs, and filling him with a strength he had never before known. Those who are evil can tap into a sinister well of strength, but those who love, have the whole universe behind them. Ten years of lost love had nearly killed him, but that was over. Now was the only moment that mattered, and now was flooded with the power of love. Ernie struggled to sit up, his head ringing. Then, for the first time since the ambulance had shattered his pelvis and broken his legs, he got to his feet without the help of his crutches.

"Bloody hell," he exclaimed, but did not have any time to enjoy this miracle.

o o o

Goliath lurched towards Ernie his face contorted into a ball of hatred.

"Enough of this," Ernie muttered, fumbling with his trouser belt. Drawing his pistol, he pointed the muzzle at Goliath's chest. The monster froze.

"Those were my kids you just terrorised, and the mother of my children you hit in the face. Now you are going to pay for it."

Goliath said nothing.

As Ernie's index finger slowly tightened on the trigger, he imagined the bullet ripping through Goliath's chest. He saw the giant stumble and hit the ground. He saw the tiny, red bullet wound in Goliath's heart, and the fist shaped hole in his back. It did not feel good. Revenge was not a dish Ernie ever wished to serve, even to an evil man. Looking over at his boys standing in the doorway of their home, shaking. He knew he could not execute a man in front of his own children. He was in a brutal dilemma. If he hesitated for much longer Goliath would sense his weakness, and then it would all be over. Ernie noticed Karen in the background struggling to get to her feet. As if sensing what was going on, she hurried the boys into the safety of the house.

"Ah should blow your brains out right now, but that'd be too good for you, you wife beating son of a bitch," Ernie threatened, "but ah'm not going to." With a gulp, he tossed the pistol away and straightened up to face Goliath, unarmed.

As a gleeful Goliath grabbed him, Ernie twisted to one side, breaking Goliath's grip. He was quicker than the big man and punched him as hard as he could on the jaw. Goliath hardly noticed. Ernie already regretted his choice. Like a gnat fighting a bear, he started to take a pounding. Punch, after head butt, after kick, rained down on his small body, as the giant mocked him mercilessly.

"Come on ya little shit. Is that all you've got?" he goaded. Both of Ernie's eyes opened up, and blood began streaming down his face. His nose was flattened, and his ribs stung. Ernie Manning was in the process of being beaten to death. With a mighty hand, Goliath grabbed Ernie's head and rammed it onto the pavement.

Smash.
Crunch.
Squelch.

Ernie mustered all of his strength to look up through a mass of blood and tears. All he could see was his thuggish opponent looming over him. Goliath looked like a striker about to take a penalty kick in the F.A. Cup final. The giant's boot came flying in and instinctively Ernie ducked to one side. Goliath lost balance as his foot met with thin air, and Ernie threw all of his remaining strength into a right cross.

Thump!

Goliath groaned, clutching his crotch. His face contorted with pain as he went down on one knee. Kneeling beside him, with his head bowed, Ernie's world slowed down as one of his underwater moments enveloped him. He felt so peaceful. It would not take long for Goliath to recover and finish Ernie off, but he was not concerned. He felt calm, resigned to his fate. The fear of losing, the fear of Goliath, even the fear of death had melted away. Ernie had given it his best shot, he had played his cards as best he could, and knowing this he could die in peace.

"Ah gave it my best shot," he whispered, through the blood dripping from his mouth. The rain continued to pour down, and thunder cracked overhead, as if nature herself knew the significance of what was happening below. Goliath grunted and forced himself to get to his feet. His gaze turned towards the little man who was now so close to death. Goliath's fists tightened, and his scowl deepened. Even a man as cruel as he had to prepare himself before he killed in cold blood.

Finally, he was ready. Now it was time for Ernie to die.

o o o

Ernie's face was warm and wet. He had no idea if it was blood or rain, probably both. His sense of tranquility was so deep that it did not matter anyway. Through the fog of his beaten brain, a woman's voice broke the silence. The voice was faint, but familiar.

"To your right, reach to your right," it instructed. Without thinking, Ernie stretched out his hand and felt nothing but the cold crunch of gravel on his fingers. "A bit further Ernie, you've nearly got it. Stretch a bit further," encouraged his mother's voice. Goliath bent forward and grabbed Ernie's hair, eyeing the slim neck he was about to break.

This was it.

With great effort Ernie stretched his arm a little further.

Nothing.

Then a little further.

"Thank God," he thought, as he felt the hard metal of the Glock touch his fingers. He tried to pick it up but his grip failed, and the weapon slipped from his

grasp.

Goliath did not notice the gun. The red mist had come down, and nothing was going to stop him. He tugged at Ernie's hair lifting the little man's head up to face him, preparing to snap his neck like a chicken.

"You bastard. I hate you," screamed Karen and Goliath wheeled around. Karen was running towards him brandishing a kitchen knife, her nose bloody and her lips cracked.

"I'm not going to let you kill my Ernie," she shouted, filled with the same love fueled courage that had got Ernie into so much trouble.

Goliath looked at her like a hungry hammerhead looks at a shoal of tuna, but although she had no chance against him, Karen bought Ernie a few seconds of time. Using what felt like his last ounce of strength, Ernie grabbed the weapon.

"Oh shit."

"Got it."

Bang.

Goliath let go of Ernie's hair. His hollow eyes staring at the bloodied, little man kneeling next to him. For a second Ernie thought Goliath might ignore the bullet and keep on coming, but not even this beast of a man could survive a head shot at point blank range. The big man swayed from side to side, his eyes rolled up into the top of his head, he fell backwards, and was dead before he hit the ground.

o o o

Karen stumbled over to Ernie, still holding the kitchen knife in her shaking hand.

"I never knew I'd taught you to fight so well," she said, trying to sound brave but trembling as they embraced. "Where the hell have you been? I've been waiting years for you to come back," she whispered in his ear as she pulled him closer.

"Ouch, pet, you're ganna' break me ribs, like," Ernie moaned, and they both exchanged nervous giggles. Some things never change.

"I thought he was going to kill you."

"It feels like he did."

"You look good, kind of. A bit of blood, broken lips, busted up face, I think it's an improvement," Karen teased. Ernie glanced over to Goliath's body.

"Ah didn't want to kill him," he frowned.

"You had to, or he would have killed both of us."

"It's becoming a bit of a habit these days."

Another crack of thunder smashed the silence above them, and they instinctively clung tighter to each other. Two drowned rats, grateful for being alive and grateful that they had found each other once again.

o o o

Karen kissed Ernie on the forehead, pulled herself away and walked towards the twins who were now standing in the doorway.

"It's okay. It's all going to be okay," she said reassuringly as she hugged them. "Liam, Noel, I want you to go inside and make yourselves some biscuits and milk. Make sure you stay in the kitchen until I come and get you, okay? And close the door, I'll be with you in a few minutes." The boys nodded in unison their faces white with shock.

Dragging Goliath's body into the basement inch by inch was exhausting.

"Alive or dead, this bastard has just about killed me," Ernie moaned, as he collapsed into a battered old armchair in Karen's living room.

"Today hasn't turned out that well, has it?" Karen sighed.

"Not really. How the hell am ah going to get away with murder, like?"

Dusk had fallen and the thunderstorm had kept

the neighbours inside. There was a chance that no one had seen the fight or heard the shot, and if they had, no one would want to get involved.

"In Byker the neighbours mind their own business, particularly when it involves Dave," said Karen.

"Ah feel like ah went ten rounds with Mike Tyson," Ernie groaned, as he leaned his head over the back of his chair. Ignoring her own wounds, Karen fetched some cotton wool, surgical spirit and plasters from the kitchen and began to patch Ernie up.

"Ow, easy, pet," he winced. The pain worsening now he had time to think about it.

"Ow, ow," he complained, but Karen's attention made the pain almost worthwhile.

"For goodness sake Ernie, I'm hardly touching you, you big baby," Karen scoffed.

"Well, ah may be a bit soft around the edges, like, but as for your taste in men. A bit on the dodgy side, don't you think?" Ernie teased as she cleaned the blood off his head with a towel.

"I'm not the one who looks like an extra from the Living Dead," Karen replied, pressing a little harder on his wounds.

"Ow, ow, ow."

Karen stopped dabbing and gazed into Ernie's eyes.

"I missed you."

"I missed you, too."

"I thought about you every day. Every day for ten years! Where have you been, Ernie?" Karen threw him a look that was somewhere between love, anger and disbelief.

"It's a long story, pet."

"Mine's a long story too. I hope you're going to hang around long enough so we can tell each other our stories?" she asked, a knot of concern tightening in her chest. "You are staying, aren't you?"

"Ah was hoping you'd ask me that. Yes, ah came here to find you, ah'm not going anywhere without a fight."

"I think you've had enough fights for today," she replied.

o o o

Full of emotions that she did not understand, Karen told Ernie the brief version of the last decade of her life. She told him about having the twins, losing Rex and Aunt Rose, and ending up on the street. Ernie listened patiently, wishing he could have been there for her. Ernie then recounted the story of his arrest, prison, heroin and life on the street, glossing over his months working for the Fat Man. Their shared suffering strengthened the lovers' bond which turned into something far deeper, something that could last forever, if only life would give them that chance.

"Oh my God, Ernie. We never left each other. We lost each other," gasped Karen in amazement.

"Who was that psycho?" Ernie interrupted.

"He's called, I mean, he was called Dave. He was in with some bad people," Karen replied, her mind returning to the single shot to Dave's head that she had witnessed only minutes before.

"Anyone ah know?"

"I don't think so. He worked for a guy in London, someone really heavy. Someone who scared him a lot, and no-one scared him."

"A guy in London, eh? D'you know his name, like?" Ernie asked nervously.

"Some posh businessman. Apparently he never goes north of Watford, says the women are too ugly."

Ernie's stomach churned.

"Now what was he called?" Karen thought out loud. "Dave never liked talking about business, but I remember he told me, everyone called him..."

She paused to think.

"What? What did they call him?" asked Ernie, his head spinning.

"They called him. No, it's gone."

Then she remembered.

"The Fat Man. Yes, that's it, the Fat Man."

Ernie's head lurched forward and he threw up over the side of the chair.

"This is bad news, Kazza," he spluttered. "This is really bad news. We've gotta get out of here, we're in big trouble."

"We have to call the police Ernie. It was self-defense. We can tell them the gun was Dave's. We can work this out, can't we?"

"No, Kazza, we can't. We won't be safe from the Fat Man, even if we are locked up. He owns the frigging police. We've got to run, and we've got to do it now."

Karen shot him a worried look.

"We need to take the boys and disappear for a while. Ah've got a plan," Ernie lied, laying a comforting hand on her knee. "Go and get the boys packed. We've got to leave in five minutes."

The kitchen door opened and the twins, whose curiosity had got the better of them, hesitantly walked into the living room with milk moustaches on their upper lips. They watched Ernie with wide eyes, keeping a safe distance as he pulled himself out of the chair and nodded to them.

"Hello, ah'm Ernie," he told them, like a businessman introducing himself to two potential clients.

"Relax, they won't bite you," Karen told him,

and he laughed, revealling a bloodstained set of teeth. The boys took one look at Ernie's bloody face and backed away.

"Don't worry boys. He's a friend. Come over here and give Mummy a hug," Karen said kindly. The twins rushed over to her and held her tightly. "Liam, Noel, we're going on holiday for a while. Mummy's not quite sure where, but I need you to help me. We're going to go upstairs to play a game, ok?"

"Okay, mum."

"We're going to see how quickly we can pack your things, and then we're going on a car trip."

"Okay" they replied and ran up the stairs with Karen following close behind.

o o o

Less than half a mile from Karen's home, a sinister looking individual was stalking through the outskirts of Byker. He was slight of build and dressed in a smart, black suit, with a fop of hair smeared onto his scalp with too much gel. His tongue was slipping and sliding over his train-track braces, as his eyes darted to and fro, taking in everything like a reptile in the midday sun. No-one who valued their life would wear a suit in the toughest part of Newcastle, but this man had nothing to fear. His presence alone was strong enough to deter the most malevolent of thugs.

Whilst the Fat Man's other hitmen had dispersed to different parts of London, Spider had headed north, sensing Ernie would head for his homeland. Spider's psychic gifts made finding anyone a piece of cake, and now this Fuhrer look-a-like was closing in on his victim, licking his lips and hissing quietly to himself.

His abilities had made him the most sought-after hit man in the South East. No one knew how he did it, but it was said he could put his mind anywhere he chose and watch anyone doing anything at any time. In the Underworld there were rumours that Russian agents had at one time been sent to recruit him. It was said they tracked him down and offered him half a million dollars to come and work for them. Spider had refused.

A few days later they returned and offered him double. Again, he refused.

They came back a third time, and after that no one ever heard of the agents again. Spider did not like people who could not take no for an answer.

CHAPTER 17

On the Run

Ernie, Karen and the boys sat in Karen's Ford Cortina with the engine running. The smell of the exhaust mixed with the cold autumn air reminded Ernie of trips in his mother's car. Ernie turned to Karen; his expression serious.

"Karen, ah've got to ask you a question. Something happened out there that doesn't make any sense. Ah could've been imagining it, because ah got hit in the face so many times."

"What Ernie?"

"When ah tossed me pistol away, it landed in the bushes of next door's garden. It was ten feet from me, in the undergrowth, no kidding, like. Ah don't think you could've tooched it, because you were on the other side of me. You didn't tooch it, did you?"

"No, I didn't have the chance. I was too busy being knocked out."

"Ah knew it. It was her helping me," he thought, a look of amazement on his battered face.

"And another thing, like. There was a round in the chamber. Ah never keep a round in the chamber. With ma bad luck it's way too dangerous, like," he almost smiled. "Ah should not have been able to get me hands on that gun, and even when ah did, there should not have been a bullet in the chamber. That means that when ah pulled the trigger nothing should've happened, nothing."

Karen looked at Ernie with that intense gaze he had not seen for years.

"You know what, this world would be a very boring place if everything made sense."

"Ah think we got some help from one of me guardian angels, like?"

"Could be," she replied, lost in thought. "But we've got to get going," she replied, turning the ignition key. As they drove into the streets of Biker, Ernie looked upwards and silently mouthed two words,

"Thanks Mam."

To be continued...

About the author

Oliver Seligman was born in Inverness in 1975. As a twenty-three-year old he was desperate to find peace and hatched a cunning plan to get it. He decided to make as much money as he could, as quickly as possible and then buy a place on the beach in Thailand. Surely he could find peace there?

He got a job as a Salestrader in one of the most powerful Investment Banks on earth, intent on raking in the cash. However, a feeling there was something else he was meant to be doing with his life, would not leave him alone. Stressed out and bored, he eventually quit.

After four brushes with death he met a mysterious group of monks who taught him to Ascend. He became a monk himself, and now teaches others how to find peace and true happiness.

He lives in Oslo, writing and teaching meditation.

He has also written a book called, The Broker Who Broke Free, which available on Amazon.

Thanks

Thank you Hiranya for your unfailing support, endless patience and high-level editorial abilities.

Thank you Priya for producing such a great cover.

Thank you Shukri Devi for your pinpoint editing and persistent encouragement.

Thank you James, for your ruthlessly, precise proof reading; I knew never quite how bad my grammar was until you got your hands on this book.

Thank you Mike for your editing, encouragement and friendship over the years.

Thank you to my parents for encouraging me to go for what makes me happy and loving me no matter what.

Part two of "No Rest for the Wicked" is coming out in 2020.

It is called "Well, I'll be Damned."

Printed in Great Britain
by Amazon